Lucky Me

Everything I've Learned
From Life's Misfortunes

by
Lisa Brough

First Published in 2019 by Lisa Brough.
Written by Lisa Brough.
Editing by Anne Grange
at Wild Rosemary Writing.
Text and Photographs Copyright
© Lisa Brough 2019.

All rights reserved. No part of this publication may be reproduced, stored in a retrieval system, or transmitted in any form or by any means, electronic, mechanical, photocopying, recording, or otherwise, without the prior permission of the author.

Some names and other identifying features have been changed to protect the privacy of the author and her family, friends and colleagues.

ISBN: 9781702507141

Dedication

I would like to thank all the wonderful and inspiring people I have met throughout my journey in life. These people have influenced me and made me the person I am today.

A special big thank you to Paul and Daniel, who are always there, no matter what.

*My wonderful Nanna and Grandad
– with me as a toddler.*

Contents

Dedication i
Preface iv
Chapter 1: Childhood 1
Chapter Two: School Days 22
Chapter 3: Working Girl 30
Chapter 4: Gary 46
Chapter 5: Back Home 61
Chapter 6: Adam 69
Chapter 7: A New Millennium 82
Chapter 8: Holiday Antics 90
Chapter 9: My Best Friends 93
Chapter 10: Life Goes On 102
Chapter 11: When Will It Ever End? 111
Chapter 12: Voldemort 116
Chapter 13: Paul 125
Chapter 14: Gypsy Woman 139
Chapter 15: Mr Smith 143
Chapter 16: Goodbye Dad 148
Chapter 17: The Priory & The Flat from Hell . 157

Chapter 18: Hanbury 163
Chapter 19: For the Love of Dogs 168
Chapter 20: Up, Up and Away!...................... 183
Help and Advice..187

Preface

I decided to tell my story because when people knew my circumstances and the incidents that have happened to me, they would say: *'You should write a book'*. In some cases, they would look at me with a sceptical expression as if to say: *'Yeah, really? And you're still smiling?'*

The main reason for writing this book is for you. If you are in a similar situation, hopefully you will realise that you can get through anything and live the life you want. Just stay strong.

I was lucky. I had my family to help and support me, but I know that there are many people who think that they are alone in dealing with their problems. But you are not alone. There are lots of places where you can go for help, support or just where someone will listen to you. You just need to make that first step.

When I was younger, you'd have to really search for information to find help. Now, organisations and charities can easily be found on the internet. Also, there are more laws around coercive relationships, which have been introduced fairly recently. If those laws had been in place earlier, they would have helped me a lot. But women (and men) are still being hurt and killed in abusive circumstances.

Even now, for example, when Paul reassures me that Gary can't do anything to me, that fear is still instilled in me, because it was a constant fear. The fear doesn't switch off; it's there all the time. It's just a matter of learning to live with it.

Writing down and reliving my life again for this book has not been easy. It has bought a lot of sad and horrible memories back, but also some good ones too – of family and friends. I still live and cope with mental health problems but I've learnt that it's nothing to be ashamed of and you should never be afraid to ask for help.

If only one person finds the strength and courage or gets the help and support they need from reading this book, then I will have achieved my aim in telling my story.

Best Wishes
Lisa x
October 2019

Chapter 1: Childhood

'If it wasn't for bad luck, we wouldn't have any luck at all.' That was one of my Nanna's many sayings – she told us a lot of them as I was growing up. It's not until now that I realise how much logic and meaning there is behind these proverbs. I miss my Nanna; she was one special, unique person. Not only was she like a second Mum, but she was my best friend.

We saw her every day and she was there for us, no matter what, not just for me but for anyone. My Nanna was the one you went to if you had any problems or felt ill. She would make you feel better with her words of wisdom and her herbal remedies. My uncle's friends would even come to consult her about what was best for their greyhounds.

If she lived in the 15th century, she would have been burned as a witch.

I used to love to listen to the stories and tales she told me about when she was growing up.

My Nanna didn't have much of a life. Her mother died when she was very young and one of her sisters died of TB. Her father remarried not long afterwards, to a woman that she and her siblings called 'Mar'.

She told me she had to look after her brothers and sisters when her mother died.

In the olden days, when you left school at about fifteen years old, you were put out to work. She was sent to a big house in Buxton, to work for a rich Derbyshire family. My Nanna said it was exactly like the television programme *Upstairs, Downstairs*, which was the 1970s forerunner to the current TV drama *Downton Abbey*.

Nanna said that one of the sons of the family was always trying to corner the maids to have a kiss and fondle. The maids slept on the top floor in the attic and she said there were a few times when she barricaded herself in her room because she was scared of his advances.

She didn't like working in the big house and one day in winter, she walked all the way home with another maid, from Buxton to Holymoorside, the village where her family lived, just outside the town of Chesterfield.

When she arrived home, her father made her walk all the way back again.

She eventually met my Grandad and they got married in January 1942. She said that she only married him because it was wartime and being married meant she could stay in Chesterfield instead of being sent away to work. But I think that was one of her jokes, as Nanna and Grandad were together till they died.

My Nanna would tell me about her travels down to London during the Blitz. My Grandad was stationed there and she went to visit him. His position was on the big searchlights, watching for enemy planes in the sky. She described what it was like when the bombs fell and the sirens went off; she hid under the dining table at the place where she was staying. She said it was better under the big table than in the air raid shelters, which were cramped and full of people.

My Nanna would explain all of this in a matter-of-fact way, as though it was an everyday, normal occurrence.

My Grandad was sent to fight abroad during the D-Day landings, and while he was overseas, my Mum was born. He sent my Nanna a pair of wooden Dutch clogs with the year 1944 painted on them. I have still got them. He said there was nothing else that he could send home.

While my Grandad was patrolling the streets in Holland and Belgium, he was shot in the back. At the time, it was his job to carry the refreshment supplies for the soldiers' tea breaks. If it wasn't for the packets of tea and sugar absorbing the bullet, it would have killed him.

He was taken to the army hospital and was eventually sent home a few weeks afterwards. Years later, he still suffered from his shoulder wound, but you never heard him complain, although he still had some shrapnel lodged in his shoulder.

My Nanna also told me tales about the times when my Grandad was drunk and pinned her up against the wall by her throat.

She said that the doctor gave her some tablets to put into my Grandad's tea to help calm him down. She didn't know what they were but she said they did the trick. My Nanna would stand in the kitchen, stirring the cup of tea to dissolve the tablet and start to panic because it wasn't disappearing fast enough and was frightened my grandad would see it.

But my Grandad was always okay with me. He never raised his voice or anything.

'How's my Leela?' he would always ask.

That was his pet name for me. I think he was kinder towards me because I respected him, unlike my brother and sister, who never had time for him or once sat down and listened to what he had to say.

I loved to listen when Grandad spoke about the past, just like I did when Nanna told me stories. He didn't talk very much but when he did, I would listen.

Grandad would mention odd things, like when he was a soldier on the searchlights and the air raid sirens went off. He said that the American soldiers would run and hide. He would never speak about the violent shooting or his lost comrades, although he spoke very highly of the Red Cross and the NAAFI (the Navy, Army, and Airforce Institute), who made a good cup of tea.

You can learn a lot from the older generation, if you just take the time to listen. You never know how long you've got to learn from them.

My Grandad was later diagnosed with hydrocephalus (water on the brain). Some of the symptoms are similar to dementia. He would still think I was at school, even when I was in my thirties, and would often think that I was my Mum.

Sadly, he died in 2004, aged 84.

My uncles were both characters too.

My uncle Tony lived with my Nanna. He had been married but got divorced after a few years. I was only very young at the time, so I can't really remember his wife. He had two boys, Robert and Ryan. They would visit us at the weekends and stay for a couple of weeks during the summer holidays.

We would play outside, making our own entertainment, going out on bikes, taking the dogs for walks and making climbing frames with milk crates stacked on my Nanna's back yard. In autumn, we would go "conkering". We weren't like kids today, stuck inside playing on Xboxes and PlayStations.

Tony was a milkman – hence all the milk crates in Nanna's back yard. In the holidays, we would sometimes help him on his milk round. He was known as a loveable rogue; everyone who knew him couldn't help but like him.

I remember that he once told me that I could pick apples off the trees in someone's back garden, because the owners had said that it was okay. Another time, he told me to pick a cabbage out of someone else's garden, '...and make sure it's the biggest!' Again, Uncle Tony told me that the owner knew him and that he could help himself whenever he wanted. It wasn't until many years later that I realised that this wasn't the case!

Tony did get into some scrapes and trouble, but he was harmless.

Once he got caught pinching doors off a council site. He appeared in the local paper, the *Derbyshire Times*. The headline was 'Milkman has a lotta bottle'. Tony used his milk van to steal the doors. The best bit though, was that the doors he took were no good for anywhere else, because they were extra-wide doors for disabled people's houses!

Before he was a milkman, he was a bus driver – even then, he got into a few scrapes.

He was driving a double decker bus one day and went up towards Whittington hill. There's a bridge there and somehow, he forgot he was driving a double decker and he ripped the top off the bus. It was a good job that no one was on the top deck and very lucky that nobody was hurt.

My uncle Mike, who is my Mum and Uncle Tony's younger brother, was also married but got divorced later. He has twins called Jane and Andrew.

He was a plumber by trade and for a few years, he worked for my brother until they fell out and he upped and left Chesterfield, I've not seen him since. He was a gambler and conned my brother out of a lot of money. He got into debt through his gambling.

Both of my uncles were into greyhound racing and both kept greyhounds. They would sometimes take us kids down to the dog track called Wheeldon Mill at Brimington, Chesterfield. It has since been demolished, and houses are being built there now.

There was a lot of wheeling and dealing in dog racing, and my uncles knew all the tricks.

They would have a really good fast dog and do the trails and races with it. But then, just before a particular race, when everyone would bet on it because they knew it was good and fast, my uncles would feed the dog condensed milk. This slowed the dog down and my uncles would bet on the next best dog, which usually belonged to their friends.

Another trick my uncles played was to swap a dog that wasn't very good for one that was really fast. But each racing greyhound had a number tattooed in its ear. To convincingly switch the dogs, they asked my Dad to paint some white on the dog's tail. Both dogs were all-black, but the fast one had a splash of white on its tail. Also, my Dad had to alter the number on its ear.

They asked my Dad because he was an artist and painted pictures, so of course he was classed by my uncles as an expert dog painter too!

When Dad had finished, my uncles asked my Nanna to go into the back yard and see if she could tell the difference. She went outside and looked at the dogs.

'Yes, they look alike,' she said.

My uncles were pleased.

'The only trouble you've got is that one's a bitch and one's a dog. How are you going to sort that out?' Nanna said as she turned to go back inside.

As far as I know, they still got away with it.

There is many a tale I could tell you about my uncles.

My uncle Malcom, who is my Dad's younger brother, never got married and lived with my Grandma at Staveley. He still lives there now. I don't really remember my Grandad. I was only two years old when he died in 1973, aged only 59.

My Grandma died in 2005, aged 90.

I feel sorry for uncle Malcom, as my Grandma ruined his life.

When he and my Dad were very young, they had an older brother called Trevor, but he died when he was aged eighteen.

Trevor was conscripted into National Service and was posted to RAF Padgate. He committed suicide; he was found hanging. He had unpicked the cord from his duffle bag and hung himself from the rafters in his dorm. They think he was being bullied, as this camp was well known for it and after a while it was closed down; apparently a couple more cadets had committed suicide.

My Grandma was never the same again.

Malcom didn't cope well either and stopped going to school, so the school police came and took him away to an Approved School, which was a bit like a boarding school.

A couple of years ago, Malcolm told me that one of the teachers there had been abusing some of the boys, physically and mentally, and that there was a big enquiry into it, involving the police and solicitors.

Malcom worked as a gardener at Renishaw Hall for a number of years. In fact, Malcom knew the Sitwell family very well and that's how my Dad got one of his paintings exhibited in Renishaw Hall gallery for the public to see.

My Dad was the middle child and he had a tough childhood, with his older brother Trevor committing suicide when Dad was only fifteen, and Malcolm, his younger brother, being sent away to an abusive Approved School.

When Dad was a just a young kid, he got into trouble for throwing a handful of sand at his brother. My Grandma beat him with a leather belt. She was so mad and hysterical; she got the wrong side of the belt and hit my Dad several times, with the buckle end around his head.

My Dad was unconscious and when he came around, he was in his bed and the family doctor was there. He said that he could remember the doctor saying to my Grandma that she had gone too far this time and he should really report her. The doctor threatened her and told her never to do it again.

As far as I know, I don't think Grandma did anything like that to him again, but she didn't really have much to do with my Dad. It sounds like he was virtually left to fend for himself, while my Grandma was gossiping over the fence with the neighbours all the time.

We think this is why my Dad was partially deaf in one ear.

He wasn't very good at school but he was a natural artist, and the teachers encouraged him by asking him to paint murals on the school walls. When he left school, he found a job in London, painting scenery in theatres but my Grandma put a stop to it and my Grandad got him a job with the local council, painting and decorating houses in and around Chesterfield.

He met my Mum at the Vic dance hall in town. This was a popular place in the 1960s, where all the young people would go to dance and meet.

At the time, my Mum was working at Wigfields in the offices, after she had finished her education at Tapton House School.

After courting for a couple of years, they got married in October 1965 and lived at 16, Canal Wharf, Stonegravels.

In November 1968, my sister Sally came along, and then in June 1971, they had me.

I was born Lisa Anne Skingle at my Nanna's house, 48 Lucas Road, Newbold. I was born at my Nanna's house because my Mum and Dad were staying at my Grandparents' house until I arrived, to make sure my

Mum was alright when Dad was at work at night. She'd also done this before my sister was born.

We lived at Canal Wharf up until I was about two years old.

The biggest memory I had of this house was from Christmas time. My sister and I made a play shop out of a huge cardboard box, like a Wendy house. Dad would play with us and he acted as different customers. My sister always had to be the shopkeeper.

Around this time, we had a dog called Simba. He was just like the dog from the film *Lassie* and he was afraid of thunderstorms. He would run upstairs and hide under the bed or up in the attic.

Mum didn't like this house – she discovered we had rats in the attic, which is where we kept our toys. Mum threw them all away because of germs from the rats.

When Dad was on night shifts, Mum would put me and my sister in bed with her and pull the chest of drawers up against the bedroom door. She was afraid that the man at the end of the street could get in via the attic.

Canal Wharf was a row of terraced houses and all the attics and lofts joined together and went straight through from one end to the other. One night, Mum woke up and was sure she saw a man at the bottom of the bed. By the time she was fully awake, she wasn't sure what she'd seen, but it scared her.

For most of my childhood and teenage years, we lived at 19 Dowdeswell Street, which was a big Victorian house.

It had high ceilings and still had the original moulded and carved covings.

We lived in the end house at the bottom of the street, next to a big field, where the new Abercrombie Primary school is now.

We were always playing on the field with the other kids in the neighbourhood; sometimes my Mum and her friend Janet would join us in playing rounders or cricket.

If any kids had an accident on the field, they would always come to our house and Mum would take them home or to the hospital, depending how serious the injuries were.

Everyone enjoyed bonfire night and helped out with making the big fire on the field. Parents contributed towards food and fireworks. At Christmas time, carol singing and sledging happened on the field.

The community stuck together and you could play out safely on the street and leave your doors unlocked.

My brother Jon was born on Boxing Day 1980 while we lived here.

So not only did we celebrate Christmas Day, with all the family for dinner at our house, but on Boxing Day, they all came over again to celebrate Jon's birthday.

We never had babysitters when Mum and Dad went out to work. My Nanna always looked after us. Mum and Dad would work shifts that fitted in with each other – my Dad would do nights and my Mum would work on weekends. They fitted it around us children.

My Dad and Mum both worked at Lamp Caps Ltd and British Thomson-Houston engineering companies (BTH) on Sheffield Road. Then my Dad went to work at Markham & Co Engineering.

My Mum had several different jobs over the years to fit around us. Amongst other things, she worked as a cleaner at Scarsdale Hospital, as a Home Help, and her last job was working in the offices at Chesterfield Co-op.

I think the reason why I was shy and quiet was because I was the middle child. My sister always wanted to be the centre of attention and my brother was a lot younger, so he needed more looking after, especially as he suffered with eczema and asthma.

I think Sally would have liked to have been an only child. She only wanted to play with me if there were no other kids to play with. You don't realise these things when you're young, but I had to do everything she wanted to do.

Sally never had much to do with Jon when he was young either. When Mum asked if we would like a baby brother or sister, I said 'yes' straight away, but my sister said 'no'.

I can remember wanting to help my Mum to look after Jon. I would walk up and down the street, trying to get him to sleep in his pram. As he got older, Jon would sit beside me while I did my homework, wanting to use my paper and pens. Sally was always out with friends and at youth clubs. She always acted as if she didn't want me to be around.

I have lots of fond memories of living at Dowdeswell Street. However, there was an incident involving Jon while was playing on the field with his friends. Something happened to him involving two older boys, but I can't remember the exact details.

We moved house not long after this. I was about sixteen years old at the time.

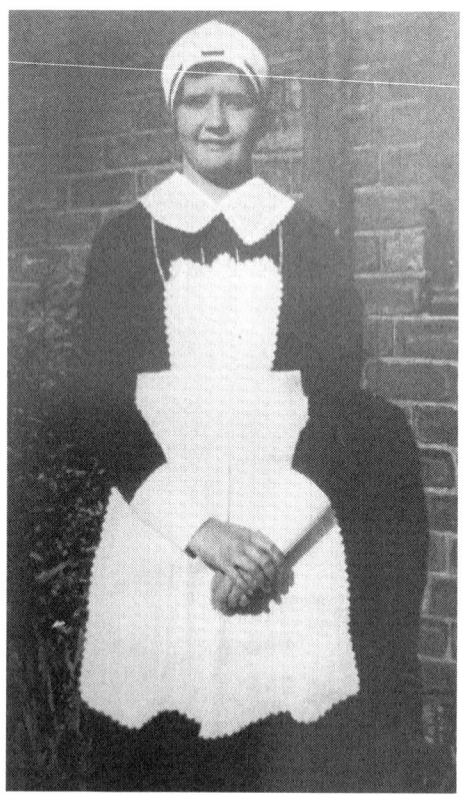

Nanna in her maid's uniform.

Nanna and Grandad in 1942, the year they married.

Mum as a girl, with her brothers Tony and Mike.

Uncle Tony was quite a character.

Nanna and Grandad in the 1970s.

Grandma Skingle in her back garden.

Grandad Skingle looking dapper.

Uncle Malcolm, who was a gardener at Renishaw Hall.

Mum and Dad's wedding day in Chesterfield.

Mum and Dad in the wedding car.

Me as a baby with my sister Sally.

Sally and me as toddlers, in matching dungarees!

A photo booth snap of me and Sally with baby brother Jon.

I loved having a baby brother to look after!

Sally, me and Jon in a family portrait.

Chapter Two: School Days

I attended Abercrombie Primary School on St. Helen Street, which was at the top of our road. I went to school here from the age of five to eleven years of age. It was only a small school. All the staff were friendly, helpful and went out of their way to help and support you. Everyone knew each other. Even now, when I see my old teachers, they recognise me and still know my name after all these years.

I was a bit of a loner, but I did make friends. I was shy and withdrawn until I got to know other children. Even at an early age, I didn't like attention or people watching me.

School plays were a nightmare for me but the teachers made sure everyone was involved and had a part in the Christmas play. And that included me. I can remember being cast as an angel once, wrapped in a bed sheet, which was okay as I could stand at the back of the others onstage and hide.

Sports day was the same. I enjoyed sports and games, especially netball and rounders. They always put me in running races because I was tall, with gangly legs, so they thought I would be good at running. I was, but I preferred netball.

In the classroom, I was sort of in the middle group. I was clever, but not clever enough to be on the top table, and I was too clever for the bottom table. Looking back now, it seems that even then, I didn't really fit in anywhere.

Swimming was made compulsory and it was on Monday mornings. I hated it. I couldn't swim and still can't. I'm terrified of water. We went by coach every Monday morning after registration, to the Manor School Baths on Ashgate Road.

The swimming instructor was called Mr Hardwick and he was a horrible man. If you couldn't swim after the first couple of lessons, then you were a waste of space to him. The floats that were used to help beginners would be literally thrown at you, hitting your head when you were in the water.

If your head was not submerged in the water, he would push it in, using a long pole with a hook on the end. This was supposed to be used to open the big, high windows that couldn't be reached by hand, but Mr Hardwick found another use; one that he found great pleasure in. He would shove the pole at the back of your head with the hook end, to push your head in the water while attempting to swim. Not surprisingly, I was terrified.

I started to pretend to be ill on Monday mornings so I didn't have to go to school and would miss the dreaded swimming lessons, and some weeks I would "forget" my swimming kit.

My class teacher and my Mum soon realised what was happening. I didn't say anything about Mr Hardwick, I just said that I didn't like swimming. I had to go to the headmaster's office with my Mum and was told that I had to go swimming.

The next time I went swimming, my teacher, Mr Lewis came into the water with the kids and he took the time to help me to swim – a bit.

One day in assembly, awards and certificates were given out and I had to go and collect my beginner's certificate for swimming. Others were collecting bronze, silver, and gold awards but on that day, I got the biggest applause and cheers from all the staff because they knew how hard it was for me to achieve it.

That's how the school was. They knew each pupil's individual needs and personalities and would try their hardest to encourage every child to do their best.

After leaving primary school in 1982, I went to Violet Markham Secondary school.

I had to go to Violet Markham because my sister was already going to this school and my Mum thought that Sally would be able to keep an eye on me. But it was just the opposite. My sister ignored me and didn't want anything to do with me. It was a good half-hour walk from our house to the school and we walked it whatever the weather: rain, sun or snow.

I was overwhelmed by secondary school and didn't like it. I was one of only three pupils who went to that school from Abercrombie Primary, so I didn't know anyone.

I did make friends with a girl called Lynn Shepherd because I sat next to her on the first day, as we had to sit in alphabetical order.

After two years, you could leave Violet Markham and go to St. Helena School because they had a sixth form. It was an all-girls' school. The boys could choose to leave and go to Chesterfield boys' school.

I didn't go, and once again, I was on my own. I was the only girl in my form not to switch to St. Helena School. So I was put into another form group and I had to make friends all over again. Except that everyone had already made friends over the past couple of years, so I was the odd one out yet again.

It took a while before I made friends with a girl called Louise and a small group of others: Claire, Sharon, Lynn, Dawn, Claire, Jenny, Debbie and Donna.

I was friends with Louise for about a year, but then she started to fancy a bloke who lived across the road from her. He was in his late teens or early twenties and had a car. Louise wanted me to go out with his friend. I said no.

That's when she started being nasty to me, spreading rumours around school that I was gay. Louise started hanging around with another girl and they spent all their time talking about what they got up to with the two boys. The other girl ended up pregnant.

Eventually, my whole group of friends, and then the entire class, started to pick on me or completely ignore me. So I had no friends; no one to turn to. I didn't tell anyone – I felt so alone.

That's when I started to self-harm. I would sit in class and scratch my hand or arm with the end of a compass, or anything sharp in my pencil case. It was like a release. I was bottling everything up; I didn't know how to cope. It was like a distraction, a control mechanism and maybe, deep-down, I was punishing myself.

I didn't realise what the word self-harm meant until a few years ago when I was watching an episode of Emmerdale on TV which featured a storyline about a character called Aaron Dingle, who was self-harming by cutting himself, and running to make himself ill.

When I was younger, this sort of thing was never talked about or shown on TV, and there were no help lines or places to go. Now there are websites, support groups and chat lines.

I hated myself. I'd had little confidence before the bullying had started and now I felt even less confident. I felt that I was ugly, stupid, horrible and worthless.

I started to make myself ill so that I didn't have to go to school, or I would go to school and then leave straight after registration. I got into trouble about it on several occasions.

I would skip meals, or I would try to drink cleaning fluids and bleach to make myself ill. I would sneak downstairs in the middle of the night and go through the cupboards to see what I could find. This is when I also started taking paracetamol tablets in large doses. I've recently discovered that this is also a form of self-harm.

I was really withdrawn; I didn't talk to anyone and sat alone at school. When I was at home, I stayed in my bedroom all the time and didn't go out. I just listened to music or read books. I spent most of my time with my Mum, Nanna and my brother.

At parents' evening in the last year of school, a teacher told my Mum and Dad that I had been bullied but that it looked like I had handled it well on my own. This was the first my Mum knew of it and she then realised why I wouldn't go to school.

'Why didn't you say anything?' Mum asked me.

'I don't know,' I replied, upset.

'I'm mad with them, not you,' she said.

There were no anti-bullying campaigns, helplines or organisations to help the victims of bullying back then.

In the last year of school, that group of girls wanted to start talking and being friends with me again – because they liked the boys in our class and some of the boys were still talking to me and let me sit on their table in classes.

Looking back on the situation now, they obviously thought that by being nice to me, they could get closer to the boys they fancied. I started talking to those girls again, but I never will forget how they treated me.

I guess my experience at school is the reason I don't make friends easily. I'm afraid that the same will happen again and it's hard to trust anyone.

I did sit my exams and I did quite well, considering all the time I'd had off from school. I had originally wanted to be a vet, but after the bullying, I didn't want to go to college, so the careers team at school were basically not interested in me.

In June 1987, I left school and went out into the big wide world to find a job by myself.

Class photograph from Abercrombie Primary School. I'm on the back row, second from the right.

My class at Violet Markham Secondary School. I'm one of the tall ones at the back, third from the right.

Chapter 3: Working Girl

I applied for several jobs but without any luck, so I ended up on a Youth Training Scheme, which was the government's idea to make the unemployment figures look good in the 1980s.

In other words, it was slave labour for the young school leavers who couldn't find jobs and were not allowed to sign on at the social.

I worked all week, full time for £27.50. In the second year, if you lasted that long on the scheme, it went up to £35 a week.

One day a week, I went to a training centre and did written work and tests with other trainees, which got you a City and Guilds qualification.

My placement on this scheme was in a sweet shop called Rainbow in Chesterfield town centre. I was there for about six months. I didn't like it because you weren't allowed to talk when the boss was there and all I did was fill the sweet containers up all day.

I left and was sent on another placement, in a shop called Card and Cakecraft which was in Theatre Yard, in the town centre. I liked working there – the other staff were really friendly and nice. I learned a lot from the manageress, Lena. She showed me how to make sugar flowers, make wedding bouquets and fancy cake making and decorating.

The owner, Jill, also had other shops, one in the Market Hall, a stall on Chesterfield market and a portacabin on Beetwell Street.

We didn't use a till, so we had to add up in our heads or use a bit of paper and pen – sometimes it was challenging, especially when a customer was buying lots of individual cake decorations.

At the end of the two years, Jill kept me on and I was paid £40 a week for full-time work.

Part of my job was taking stock, money and helping out from one shop to the other, so I walked from Theatre Yard to the portacabin most days. As I used to pass by, a man who owned one of the other cabins used to say hello and chat to me at odd times.

I was walking along Beetwell Street one day in summer 1988 when the man asked if I would watch his shop for him as he needed to go to the town hall, saying something about paying his rent for the shop. I agreed to mind his shop in my dinner hour. It became a regular thing. Sometimes he would be gone a while and at other times, he would only be gone for a few minutes.

It was a clothes shop and once he gave me a pair of jeans and another time, he gave me a short denim skirt that he insisted I wear. He said it was for helping in his shop. He told me he was from Doncaster, supposedly, and he was always asking me to go there with him after work and saying he would bring me back to Chesterfield in the morning. I kept making excuses.

I don't know why, but I was getting a bit wary and unsure about him. Looking back, he must have been already doing or saying things that I thought were strange.

I remember that he would get people calling in, mostly men, who didn't buy anything or even look around the shop. He would send me into the back room to make a drink. I would hear them whispering, and when I returned, I would feel uncomfortable, like they had shared a private joke or secret.

A police officer called in one day while I was there and at one point, they started talking in their own language (they were both Asian), so I didn't know what they were talking about.

One day, he asked me to go and make a cup of tea in the back room. While I was making the drink, I saw him lock the shop door. But I didn't think anything of it because it was half-day closing on Wednesdays.

The next thing I knew, he walked into the back store room and came up behind me and before I knew what was happening, I was on the floor with him on top of me. I don't know if I banged my head as I can't recall how it happened but he was on top of me and had my skirt up around my chest and my pants pulled down

I struggled and pleaded as much as I could. Even now, I can still remember the feeling of being trapped underneath him with his weight crushing down. I think I went into shock. I felt like I was looking down on myself; it was all happening to someone else. I was numb with shock.

He raped me several times and at one point, he tried to shove a coat hanger up inside me, which was when I felt the pain so much I started shouting and telling him to stop. He got off me. I was crying and he told me to shut up; it was my own fault, I was asking for it, just like the rest. I didn't know what he meant – I was just relieved that he'd released me and was trying to make myself decent.

He was laughing at me and saying something about me being a virgin.

'Did you enjoy it?' he asked, sarcastically. He kept taunting me, saying that I'd lost my virginity to him. He said it was a long time since he could remember what a virgin felt like.

I remember feeling dazed and weak. I couldn't stand up straight away – my legs felt like jelly. I was bleeding between my legs and it was very painful. He just stood, casually fastening his trousers and smiling with a sick, twisted grin.

I told him that I would go to the police. He laughed and said that no one would believe me because I was asking for it, plus, he had friends in the police force.

The police station was only across the road from the portacabins and I knew he did have friends there because of that policeman, called Roger, who came into his shop to talk to him.

I don't know how long I was locked in the shop but eventually, he opened the door and I went straight home.

I can recall that on my way home, I felt like everyone was looking at me and staring. I was ashamed and felt disgusting.

When I got home, I ran a hot bath straight away.

'What's wrong?' Mum asked.

'I just don't feel well,' I replied.

After a couple of weeks, I was off ill at work, and it wasn't long after that I finished working in the shop.

I never told anyone.

I was seventeen. I'd never had a boyfriend; I was very naive and I'd had a sheltered upbringing. I think I couldn't mentally process what had happened. I was in shock and denial. I just couldn't understand that something like that could happen to me.

I just remember feeling numb – like everything was happening to someone else and I was looking down on it all. I felt dirty all the time. I lost what little confidence I did have.

That's why I don't feel comfortable while wearing skirts and dresses – I feel like I'm asking for trouble as that's what I was wearing when he raped me.

I don't like doors being shut or locked – I start to panic. And I don't like people standing behind me.

He told me his name was Gupta.

Looking back now, and knowing what has been happening during the past years around Sheffield, Rotherham and Rochdale, I've begun to wonder if he wasn't part of one of those groups selling girls for sex.

Watching the news, reading the accounts of the victims and finding out how these low-lives acted, reminds me of some of the things he said and did.

After it happened, I was forever watching the news and I still do when someone is abused or raped, to see if it was him. I'm sure I wasn't the only one.

And then there comes the guilt for not reporting him and letting him get away with it to maybe do it to someone else.

And how for years afterwards, I hated myself so much for being a coward and stupid.

After I left the card shop, I was unemployed for a few months. I started to work for my Aunt and Uncle Mike, who were managing a pub on Sheffield Road called the Crown & Anchor.

My job was supposed to be looking after their twins, Jane and Andrew, who were about two at the time. But I ended up cleaning, running baths, ironing my uncle's shirts, making loads of cups of tea, making sandwiches for the football and darts team and basically being a dogsbody for them. My day off was on a Thursday but that was when my Mum looked after the twins for the day so it wasn't really a break for me.

I was told off when I took the kids out to the park, as this was because while I was out, I couldn't do all the jobs for them.

I got really fed up with them and one morning, when I turned up for work, the place looked like a bomb had hit it. There was leftover food everywhere and a sink full of pots. I walked out and went back home. Shortly afterwards, my uncle came round to see what was wrong, but he was sarcastic and said I wouldn't be happy if I worked in a joke factory. He made out that I should be honoured to be working for him. Best of all, they only paid me about £40 per week.

There's no way I would work for family again.

After being unemployed again for a few weeks, I found another job working at the Ritz video shop on Whittington Moor. It was okay there and the staff were nice too. I even went out on a works do with them around town. They looked after me because I was shy and timid.

It wasn't long before I left, because rumours were going round that the company was going to be taken over by Blockbusters and some shops would be closed, one of which was ours.

In March 1991, I got a job at the Esso Service station on Newbold Road, which was just around the corner from where I lived. In November 1987, we had moved to Mansfeldt Road, Newbold.

I also enjoyed working here; it brought me out of myself more. I would blush and go bright red when anyone started talking to me or jesting with me, but I learnt that the more I blushed, the more they would torment me and think it was funny. So I started to answer them back with witty comments. This worked most of the time, and I gained more confidence.

Even now when I get stressed or nervous, I try to make jokes and witty comments.

In May of this year, my sister, Sally, got married because she had found out she was pregnant with her new boyfriend, Tim.

I was a witness, along with Tim's brother.

For their wedding present, I made all the wedding flowers and decorations for the cake. My Dad made their wedding cake, but when they tried to cut a slice at the reception, it was like cement. It did look nice though.

My nephew was born in September and they called him Steven.

Also this year, I met a lad called David, who often came into the service station for petrol.

He asked me out and everything was okay. We would go traveling around the Peak District on our days off work and we got on really well.

I had been out with another lad called Ian a year before while I was unemployed, who worked with my Dad. In fact, my Dad set us up on a blind date. Ian was quiet and shy like me. We got on very well but he acted more like a brother. He would spend all day with me and my family and when I started work, he would be there waiting outside the shop and wouldn't go home until I said I was going to bed.

He was there every minute of the day. I was feeling a bit suffocated and needed some time on my own. In the end, I finished with him.

I had been going out with David for a few months. I felt safe with him. But then he started to want more intimacy, which I could understand but I started to get scared because of what had happened to me before. In the end, I explained to David that I had been raped and that I was sorry but I needed to take things more slowly.

He said he understood and was really sympathetic. After I'd told him, I went home and told my Mum. This was the hardest thing that I have ever done. I didn't want to upset her and break her heart. Which is exactly what happened. It was a big shock to her, as you can imagine and she felt guilty that she hadn't seen anything was wrong and couldn't help me at the time.

After that night of telling David and Mum about the rape, it felt like everyone was watching me. Maybe I was paranoid, but it seemed like they were treating me differently.

My boyfriend became distant and my Mum censored things on television. When anything involving sex came on, she would quickly change channels. I felt like she was watching my every move.

I had upset my Mum. I hated myself and I had secretly started self-harming again.

It was starting to get too much for me, so Mum took me to the doctors and they referred me to the NHS mental health services at St. Mary's Gate in town, where I was offered counselling.

I went to see a lady counsellor at the St. Mary's Gate centre a couple of times, but I wasn't comfortable talking to a stranger and I don't think she helped – she made it worse. She seemed more concerned about wanting to know the name of the man who had raped me and she came across as mad at me for not reporting the rape when it had happened. She said that I could have stopped him from doing it to anyone else. I already felt guilty about that.

I started to hate myself even more and went on a guilt trip; I became obsessed with watching news reports again, reporting any rapes in the area. I kept reading the newspapers and listening to the radio. In the end, I was so stressed and guilt-ridden that I stopped watching TV and reading anything at all for months.

On Friday 20th March 1992, I went to see the counsellor again but it still didn't seem to help. I was still uncomfortable talking about my feelings and she made me feel like I was wasting her time.

She gave me another appointment to go back the following week, which I never did.

I went home and later on, I went to work.

At about 7.50pm, I was at work doing my shift. We had been fairly busy and I was restocking the shelves while it was quiet. It had gone dark and a man came in.

I went round to the counter and the man asked if I could change a £20 note.

I said yes. As I opened the till, he started to demand the money from the till. He was very agitated and had his hand in his pocket as though he had a weapon. At first I thought it was a joke, then realised it was for real, I was really scared. But I thought to myself: *shall I start with the 1p coins?*

I pressed the panic button, which was on the floor under the counter and can remember thinking: *where are the police?* It seemed like ages, but really, it was a matter of minutes. The robber ran off down Newbold Road. I didn't know what to do.

A customer came into the garage and I served him as normal, but then I blurted out that I had just been robbed. The man stared at me and at first, I thought I was joking. Then he saw my face and he couldn't wait to get out and into his car.

Then a car zoomed into the forecourt. It was plain-clothes police, and then more marked police cars appeared. They asked me what had happened and some of the officers took off after the robber while a couple stayed and took my statement and phoned my boss up to explain about the robbery. They also phoned my Mum.

Mum soon came. The first thing she did was give me a big hug. I had held myself together up till then, but I started to cry, realising what had really happened and that it could have been so much worse.

I thought that I was being punished for telling people about the rape and that I should have kept quiet. Stupid, I know, but I was so mixed up and feeling so low, I wasn't thinking straight.

I had the following day off but the day after that, I went back into work.

It was a really hard thing to do. I had flashbacks of the incident, and the first customer I served was the hardest, having to build my confidence and trust in the customers again. But I did it and it got easier each day, but it wasn't the same. I was always wary.

The boss would stay and hang around when I was on the late shifts until my Mum came round and sat with me till I locked up. This routing went on for a few weeks, until I was more confident and strong enough to be left alone.

I told everyone I was okay, but things weren't okay.

In October 1992, everything got too much for me. David had started to keep pushing me again to sleep with him. It felt like that because everything was in the open now and I was acting normally, everything was supposed to be okay again. I felt uncomfortable at home too, for the same reasons.

One day, I came home from David's and took lots of tablets, whatever was in the house. I'd just had enough. I lay down on my bed and started to cry. Then, as I started to get drowsy, I panicked.

I could hear my Nanna and my brother downstairs. I must have shouted because the next thing I knew, my

Nanna, Mum and Dad was there. They found out what I had done and while Mum phoned the doctors, my Nanna was trying to force me to drink salt water to make me sick.

Mum and Dad took me to the hospital. I was admitted on a ward and kept in overnight.

All I did was apologise and until then, I didn't know my Mum had told anybody else about the rape. My Dad said that it didn't matter but he was so upset.

'Don't do anything like it again,' he told me. Because his brother had committed suicide and he couldn't stand it happening again.

I was discharged in the morning and Mum took me home.

I told my colleagues at work and everybody else that I'd had flu.

David became really distant and suggested we had a couple of weeks break from one another.

'Yes, if that's what you want,' I said. 'But after the two weeks, don't bother coming back.'

I think this was the excuse he was looking for. A few years later, I found out that he was gay and he was probably using me as a cover-up.

The portacabin shops where my life changed forever.

The temporary shops on Beetwell Street, Chesterfield were right opposite the police station.

Raid terror for cashier

A man in his 20s fled with a small quantity of cash from a filling station on Newbold Road on Friday evening after threatening the cashier with what looked like a gun.

He had his hand in the pocket of a denim jacket and warned the woman behind the counter that he had a gun although police believe it is unlikely he was carrying a weapon.

The woman escaped unhurt from her ordeal.

He is described as being aged about 25 and was also wearing a distinctive yellow baseball cap.

Police are appealing for anyone in the Newbold Road area around 8pm who saw anything suspicious to contact them on Chesterfield 220100.

A newspaper clipping about the petrol station robbery from March 1992.

Chapter 4: Gary

I met Gary when I was working at Newbold Service station, in October 1993. He would come in and chat. He was always polite and considerate to other customers and he made me laugh.

He told me that he had recently come out of prison for doing two and half years for assault. He told me that it was self-defence and he was protecting his girlfriend at the time from another bloke. He hit him with a pick axe handle at the back of the head. The man was apparently in hospital for a few weeks. Gary said that he was a changed man and that he had now got a job and would never be going back inside again. I believed him, and when he asked me out I said yes, because I thought everybody deserved a chance.

My Mum wasn't very pleased when she found out about him because he used to live near our house in Stonegravels. She said he was nothing but trouble, which made things very awkward at home.

In January 1994, Gary wanted us to get a flat and move in together, so I agreed. We got a flat at Green Farm Close.

At first, everything was alright. But he gradually started to change. Slowly, he started to be possessive, jealous and aggressive. I wasn't allowed to talk to anyone, especially men. I couldn't go out on my own. I had to go everywhere with him and he made it so awkward at work for me that I ended up finishing my job. I didn't realise or notice how bad it was getting at the time until it was too late.

I couldn't do anything. If he did go out and leave me on my own, he would phone up to make sure I was still in the flat. I can remember that once I took the rubbish out to the bin and I heard the phone ringing. I rushed inside to answer it but it stopped just as I got to it. He phoned straight back and I answered it but he kept demanding what I had been doing and where had I been. I told him I'd been out to the bin, but he still kept on at me. And when he got home from wherever he had been, that was it – all hell broke loose.

I'd just got out of the bath, getting ready to go out one night. I don't know what I'd said that was wrong, but he picked me up, threw me back into the bath and tried to drown me – then he acted as though nothing had happened. He knew I couldn't swim and one time, he also tried to drown me in the swimming baths.

We were playing squash one day and he hit me in the face with the racket. I had a split lip and a bruised nose. I was at work the following day and nobody said anything. I couldn't eat properly for weeks. I think he did it because I was winning.

The police came to the flat a couple of times, as apparently the neighbours called them to check that I was okay – I had to say yes because Gary was standing next to me.

Once, in the bedroom, he put a stick of rock up inside me.

Another time, he stood and peed all over me and just stood there laughing.

He made me completely shave off all my body hair – everywhere. Because I wouldn't do all my private parts, he grabbed the razor and he did it. I was covered in cuts and nicks from where he had roughly shaved me.

In March of that year, I discovered that I was pregnant. I had missed my period and was being sick. I went to see my doctor and he gave me a test to do, but I didn't go back to the doctors because Gary wouldn't let me. He kept making excuses and made sure that I was too late to get to my appointments.

Also, Gary had started to get in trouble again. He said he'd lost his licence. I found out years later that he didn't even have a driving licence – he'd never passed his test! I think that's the reason why he forced me to finish my job – because I had to drive his lorry for him. He had set up his own business as a tarmac contractor, called Spire Tarmac.

Also, he was in trouble for criminal damage and threatening behaviour.

Once, the police came to the flat, looking for him. Gary hid in the kitchen. He somehow managed to crawl behind in the units near the washing machine and because they couldn't find him, they took me to the police station instead.

This was the first time I had been inside a police station, let alone a police cell. I was frightened and felt physically ill.

They shoved me into a cell; it was just like the police cells I'd seen on television: very basic, with cold walls, iron bars and a hard bed. A policewoman brought me a couple of blankets. I could see she was trying to be nice to me: she looked at me sympathetically as she handed them to me.

After a few hours, two officers fetched me and took me into a room with just a table and chairs. They shut the door. This was a disaster; I was in such a panic that I couldn't really concentrate on what they were saying. All I could gather was that they wanted me to confirm that Gary had driven to the place where he'd done the damage, as that would give them a reason to charge him. They also wanted me to act as a witness.

I was more frightened of Gary than the police. Gary had told me that he could get tapes of any police interviews about him from his solicitor. So I kept quiet, I refused to have a solicitor, because in my opinion, I had done nothing wrong.

Eventually, they let me go. It was the early hours of the morning, and I asked if I could get a lift back home.

'Sorry, it's only one way here,' one officer said, but I think he took pity on me and he did actually drive me back to the flat.

When I got there, Gary had disappeared. I don't know where he had been, but he came home later that morning asking if I'd said anything to the police and grilling me about what the police had said to me. I was just tired and weary.

Not long after this episode, I had really bad pain in my stomach. I went to the toilet and I lost a considerable amount of blood. It was really painful. I was upset and maybe, thinking back, a little relieved. I think that all the trauma and worry with Gary being wanted by the police had caused the miscarriage.

What kind of life would a little baby have had in the environment I was living in? I was struggling to cope, never mind about having to look after a baby as well.

The police eventually caught Gary. He was remanded in custody until his court date. I went to see him in Leicester prison. This was not through my own choice – he told me I had to visit him. Even though he was locked up, he could still control me because I was so scared of him. And there was always that fear of what he would do to me.

Visiting him in prison was so degrading and embarrassing. It was definitely an experience I wouldn't recommend to anyone.

Not only did I have to visit him in prison every time he asked me to, but I also had to attend all his court appearances.

I hated it; it was depressing and awful. I would have to sit about waiting, virtually all day, till it was Gary's case and then it lasted about ten minutes if that. Then they would take him down to the cells again to go back to prison.

Like any court building, it was full of the usual trouble-making characters – people who thought it was great and clever that they were there. Even the ones who were not even appearing in court would hang about inside, bragging about stuff they had done.

It reminded me of school – the kids who bunked off school and got into trouble for not attending classes, but as soon as it was the school holidays, they would be hanging around the school grounds as if they had nowhere else to go.

I didn't have any trouble from these ne'er-do-wells because they knew I was going out with Gary, and he had a reputation as being one of the hard cases, or that's the impression I got. They would say hello and try to talk to me, but I tried to keep myself to myself.

All the police knew him, and they still do if you just mention his name.

You might be wondering why I didn't leave him. One of the threats he drilled into me was that if I ever left him, he would kill me and my family, one by one. He even told me what order he would kill them in and that he would leave me till last so I could see them suffer and die.

I believed he would do it too.

He even started to sleep with a knife at the side of the bed, threatening that if I left him, he'd come after me with it. I used to dread falling asleep at night, because he might rape me. I would lie awake and could imagine myself grabbing hold of the knife and killing him. I couldn't stand the thought of going to prison. That was the only thing stopping me from doing it. He used to pretend that he was fast asleep, but I knew that if I moved, he'd be wide awake. I didn't tell anyone about the threats or the way he was controlling me.

My Mum didn't find out about these things until a few years later, because I didn't want to upset her at first.

'I don't know how you managed,' she said. 'I'd gathered some of it but I feel bad that you couldn't tell me.' She told me that she had worried that the abuse was worse in her imagination than it had been in real life, but I think if anything, it was worse. 'I bet there's more as well,' she said.

There was a lot more, but I didn't have the heart to tell her.

'You must have been strong for him not to break you,' she said.

'I don't know what kept me going,' I replied.

Luckily I had my family to turn to, but not everyone is that lucky.

By May that year, I'd had enough. I took a lot of tablets, mixed with alcohol. I thought it was the only way I could get away from him and not hurt my family.

I think everything had become too much for me: the miscarriage, breakdown of family relationships, Gary's behaviour and the feeling of being trapped and useless. Also, I found out later that he was still going to his ex-girlfriend's house.

I ended up in hospital and was really scared that Gary would find me there, and he did. Somehow, he got his ex-girlfriend to phone the hospital and pretend she was my sister, asking how I was. Later, Gary turned up at the hospital. I didn't dare to tell the nurses why I'd taken an overdose. I just made up a stupid story.

By June, life with Gary had got really bad. He was more violent and possessive: he would throw things at me, call me names, pin me up against the wall by my throat and drag me about by my hair. The back of my neck would be bruised and really hurt for days afterwards. He would shout at me until I cried, and then when I cried, he called me names and laughed. Sometimes, he got really mad with me.

I would walk with my head down so I wasn't accused of looking at other men. I watched what I said to him, and how I answered him – because I didn't want to upset him. He would shout at me and try to humiliate me and drag me around in the flat. I couldn't even go to the toilet on my own – I had to leave the bathroom door open.

These are just some of the things I had to deal with.

In July, the police were after Gary again, so we drove to Cleethorpes and went into hiding, sleeping in the back of the car at different campsites. When we started running out of money, we had to go into the arcades to try to win some money for our next meal. When we eventually had to go back to Chesterfield, it was time for his latest court appearance. He was sent to prison for a couple of months for criminal damage. I stayed at my Nanna's house while Gary was in prison.

I didn't like to be in the flat on my own, as Gary's friend kept phoning and saying he was coming round – understandably, I was scared. I didn't have any rest from Gary, even when he was locked up.

Gary still wouldn't leave me alone. He would phone me all the time, wanting to know everything I was doing. I had to write to him every day, several pages, not just one, because if I didn't do that, he would accuse me of going out without him. He would get angry and that would frighten me, because he would threaten me with what he would do when he came out of prison.

When he did come out of prison, he said he would be different and that he had changed and was sorry. It didn't last long. He got into trouble again about a month afterwards and I was arrested too and locked up overnight for questioning. I didn't know what he'd done either, until then. Then they let me go. I think it was a way of frightening me so that I would snitch on Gary.

Things were getting worse each day. I never knew what was going to happen next. I couldn't trust Gary and I had nowhere else to go. I was so frightened.

I would be driving his lorry from really early in the morning until late at night, and then I would have to do the housework. I was really tired, but if I fell asleep at night, he would kick me awake. It got so bad that I didn't know what day, month or year it was.

I was beginning to get more and more depressed and I felt like a zombie. I was just trundling along and didn't care about anything anymore.

I also found out that Gary had not been paying the rent or the bills, so we started to receive eviction notices and court orders. I didn't know about this until it was too late. Gary would fetch the post from downstairs – the post box was in the entrance hall, and then he would throw it in the bin. This was all happening at Christmas time.

We had to move somewhere else. Straight after the New Year, we moved to a house in Stanfree.

Stanfree was a small, isolated village near Clowne back then; they've built more houses now.

I felt really ill and had no interest in anything. I thought I had flu or a bug, but it turned out that I was pregnant again.

Gary went round telling everyone about it as though he was a proud father, but at home alone with him, he was horrible. I was sick all the time and couldn't eat anything. He would just laugh at me.

He argued that the baby was going to be a boy and that it was going to be called after him. I told him no: if we weren't married, the baby would have my surname. This made him mad.

He threw a Sky satellite dish at me and another day soon afterwards, he threw the remote control at me, which hit me in the face. Within a week of finding out I was pregnant, things were so bad that he tried to throw me down the stairs and even threatened to thump me in the stomach to get rid of the baby.

Gary blamed me for his violent temper, saying that I provoked him.

One night, he went down to the pub at the bottom of the road and took the car keys with him. He knew I couldn't go anywhere.

While he was gone, I decided to run away. Something had clicked and I'd just had enough.

We had a Jack Russell dog called Max, and I took him with me, because Gary used to beat the dog too. When I made a fuss of the dog, it made Gary jealous, and then he hit the dog, so I only dared to make a fuss of Max when Gary wasn't looking. He was as terrified of Gary as I was.

I promised Max that I would take good care of him from now on as we disappeared into the night.

It had been snowing and it was pretty deep. I didn't know where I was going and I only had a pound coin to my name. I was so scared, lost and tired.

I walked across some fields and found a farm cottage. I knocked on the door and asked if I could use their phone and offered them my pound coin.

'It doesn't matter about the money,' the farmer said.

I phoned my Mum to come and fetch me. I tried to tell her roughly where I was.

She came straight away. I was terrified by now, because Gary would have discovered that I had left, so I hid behind a wall in case he was driving around, looking for me.

I don't know how my Mum found me, but she did. She said that she didn't know really where she was going, but instinct kicked in and she was somehow drawn to my hiding place.

We managed to get back home, but Gary found out and came round. I was wet through, freezing cold and shivering, so Mum told me to get in the bath. I was sitting in the bath and Mum said: 'Whatever you do, whatever you hear, don't come out.'

Gary came round, banging on the front door and demanding to see me. Because it was late and he was making a noise and causing trouble, I wrapped a towel around myself and sat at the top of the stairs. Eventually, when he calmed down, I agreed to meet him the following day, just to talk to him and so that he would go away.

I could see my Mum was upset, but I didn't realise how ill I had become. Because I was pregnant, I was being sick all the time and I'd lost a lot of weight. After I'd recovered, Mum told me that she'd been really shocked to see me, because I was just skin and bone. When she saw me, I was wearing jumpers and baggy clothes. I'd lost so much weight, but because I was just living from one day to the next with Gary, it hadn't registered.

When Gary had gone, Mum put her arms around me and she started crying. I didn't know why then, but it was seeing me so skinny and the condition I was in that made her so upset.

'Even the dog was skin and bones,' Mum said. Not because he wasn't being fed, but because he was so stressed out too with living with Gary.

Early the following morning, Gary was outside my parents' house, waiting for me. We did talk, but he just kept going on, over and over again about me going back with him. I didn't trust him and I was scared of him, but I pretended to play along with him.

I agreed to meet him again later that evening, just so that I could go back to my Mum's house and get away from him. I couldn't tell him that I didn't want to be with him anymore, because of the repercussions that I knew would follow.

But he constantly phoned me and I was getting stressed out. My Mum suggested that we went to visit Aunty Irene to get out of the way for a bit.

'You've got no time to think,' Mum said. 'That's why he keeps pestering you – so you can't think'.

So we went to Aunty Irene's, and Nanna came with us too.

Aunty Irene was Nanna's sister and lived at Clay Cross. We used to visit her often when we were young. We always liked to visit her because she had proper fizzy drinks and Mr Kipling's cakes.

We stayed there for a while that day, and when we went to leave, we realised it had been snowing, but we didn't realise how deep it was. On the way home, we got stuck in the snow but we eventually managed to get going again and back to Mum's.

'We can't keep going on like this', Mum said on the way back in the car. 'Are you going back to him or not?'

'No, but he's not going to take it lightly', I replied. 'I'm frightened of what he'll do to you all.'

'Well then, we're going to fight it out, because he's not going to push you out of your home. We're going to stick up for you. We're going home.'

When we arrived home, my Dad told us that Gary had been constantly phoning up while we were out and kept calling around to the house to see where I was – and he was mad because I wasn't there.

Gary came round again and when I told him I wasn't going back to him, he started to threaten everybody.

Uncle Tony and my Grandad came round and managed to calm him down. Tony walked Gary to his mum and dad's house down the road. They thought that was it, but I knew him better.

In the early hours of the next morning, at about one o'clock, I got a phone call from the hospital to say that Gary had taken some tablets and was refusing treatment. It wasn't true – he just wanted me to go to him. I knew it was a trick.

'No, it's too late,' I told Gary. He turned nasty and started to threaten us all again, saying what he would do to us. I phoned the police and told them what was happening, and Uncle Tony came round again and stayed with us that night.

And as I had feared, Gary turned up just as the police arrived. He kicked off in a big way and he broke the front door. It took several police officers to arrest him and Gary ended up assaulting one of them.

The following morning, my Mum found a knife under the settee. My uncle had put it there in case he needed to use it.

'What are you doing with this?' Mum asked, telling him off.

I just felt really guilty because I was bringing trouble to the family and I knew it was just the start.

Chapter 5: Back Home

After I moved back home, Gary wouldn't leave me alone. Every time I left the house, he would be there. My Dad changed his shifts at work and started to work nights, so that my Mum was with me at night and my Dad was with me in the daytime while my Mum was at work.

I didn't even leave the house without my Mum or Dad being with me. I would jump at the slightest noise and I couldn't sleep at night.

Gary kept phoning the house, all day and night. So we changed the phone number, but he kept phoning Nanna's house, so she changed her number, but he kept phoning Sally. She wouldn't change her number – she thought it was some attention for her and just a game, but then when he kept constantly hassling her, she complained and got upset. In the end, she did change her phone number but we never heard the last of it.

I felt so guilty and ashamed. I blamed myself constantly and kept apologising to my family. I felt like it was my fault, as I had caused all this trouble.

I felt in the way and a failure.

Gary constantly drove up and down the street past the house at all hours of the day and night, with the car horn blaring and loud music playing.

One morning, we woke to find that my Mum's car had been paint stripped.

We had bricks thrown through the front windows.

I had nasty letters, videos and parcels sent through the post.

Dad even received a deepest sympathy card from Gary.

If I dared to go out with Mum in the car, Gary would chase us in his lorry, and he tried to run us off the road. Then Gary bought a car which was the same colour and model as Mum's, just to confuse and intimidate me.

Also, I later found out that Gary had moved back in with his ex-girlfriend.

We reported everything that happened to the police, but they soon treated us as a nuisance and basically just told us to get on with it.

According to the police, Gary was harmless and would apparently soon get fed up and leave us alone. The police informed us that he'd harassed a previous girlfriend and was known for this sort of thing.

'He'll be like that for about a year and then he'll pack it in,' they said.

He was later arrested for breaking his bail conditions, but this fuelled his anger even more.

It all came to a head on Wednesday 15th March 1995. We'd had a day of Gary driving up and down the street in his car. Later at night, about 10.30 pm, we heard something outside. It was Gary's ex-girlfriend and she was smashing up my Mum's car which was parked on the drive, next to the kitchen.

Mum went outside to try and reason with her, but she just threatened my Mum with an iron bar. The police came and arrested her. They said she looked like she was on drugs and that she also had a knife on her.

After the police had taken our statements and left, Mum phoned my Dad to tell him that she couldn't fetch him from work in the morning, but she only told him that the car tyres had been slashed, not the full extent of the damage. She said that she would tell him about what had happened when he got home from work.

We were just going back to bed at about one o'clock on Thursday morning after an already eventful night, when we heard an almighty bang. I ran to the kitchen door, finding it ablaze. Gary had fire-bombed the car, which had set fire to the house.

I dashed into the hall and phoned the fire brigade and police. My Mum got hold of my brother and the dog and dragged them straight outside. I was still on the phone, trying to explain what had happened to the emergency services. I panicked because the gas meter was on that side of the house too, so I was expecting everything to blow up.

As soon as I knew the emergency services were on their way, I ran out of the house. The three of us: Mum, Jon and me – and the dog, were huddled outside on the street, waiting for the fire fighters to arrive.

We got into trouble with the fire fighters, as we'd left the doors in the house open and apparently, we should have shut them, to prevent smoke damage. But we didn't think about that at the time. We'd just had the trauma of seeing the car being smashed up and were stressed and not thinking rationally. We just wanted to get out of the house as quickly as possible, because we didn't know what to expect next.

Early the following morning, two CID police officers came to question us about the fire and the forensic team were already on our drive.

The CID men were dressed like they had just walked out of Burton's shop window – and their attitude was also like a couple of shop dummies. As you can imagine, we were very tired and stressed out when they were asking us questions, but even we noticed how stupid they sounded:

'Where was the car when it was set on fire?'

'Was it taxed?'

'Did it have an MOT?'

As if we had deliberately fire-bombed our own car and set our house on fire because it didn't have an MOT! The car was fully taxed and had a recent MOT.

And how on earth could the car have been moved after it was set on fire? It was a burnt out shell.

This experience gave us even less hope and confidence in the police force.

The forensic officer told my Dad that it was definitely arson, and done by someone who knew what they were doing. He explained how every piece of glass in the car had previously been broken or removed so that no traces of the inflammable substance used could be detected.

Gary had been arrested as soon as the police were informed about the blaze in the early hours of the morning, but of course he had an alibi. The only reason they were keeping him in custody was because I told them I had seen him drive down our street a few minutes before the explosion. And of course, Gary was banned from driving.

He was eventually locked up and served around three months in prison for driving while disqualified. Gary gloated about this lenient sentence. While he was inside, I received a letter from him, bragging that he'd got such a short sentence for setting fire to a family car and home.

On the 23rd May, the police phoned to say that Gary was out of prison, but we had already gathered this, because he was driving up and down our street again.

On the 27th May, while shopping at the local store, we returned to the car to find it had a petrol leak. We took it to the nearest garage and they had a look and said that the petrol pipe under the car had been cut.

Once again, we were constantly phoning the police and reporting all these incidents and as you can imagine, we were terrified of what he would do next and how far he would go this time.

In June, the CID officer who had dealt with the fire at one point phoned us, and in a very sarcastic voice, told us to report only to him and that we needed witnesses in order to have a case and to get Gary arrested. He also added that we were not to provoke Gary. This was a huge insult to us, because we never spoke to Gary and we were trying our dammed hardest to ignore him. All we wanted was to get on with our lives and not to be scared to go shopping or to even sit in our home in peace.

We got so mad and frustrated with the police that we went to see the MP for Chesterfield at the time, Tony Benn, on 23rd June. Tony Benn promised to get in touch with the police superintendent to explain our situation, and said that he would try to help resolve our problems. At the time, he was one of the members of parliament who was trying to pass a law about stalking and harassment, so he was very interested in our case and promised to keep in touch.

However, the next time we visited him, Tony Benn said that he couldn't legally help me because it was a "domestic" incident. I don't know what the police had told him, but unfortunately, he didn't want to get involved personally in my case.

The CID officer called round again and said that he knew we'd been in touch with Tony Benn. He asked if we'd had any more trouble and to ignore Gary as he was on drugs and was hanging around with a very bad crowd who were always in trouble.

Of course, if this was meant to reassure us, he wasn't doing a very good job.

The damage done to Mum's car on 15th March 1995.

The kitchen was also badly damaged in the arson attack.

Family flee blaze

A Chesterfield mother and her two children had to flee their home early today (Thursday) after a fire destroyed a car on the drive and flames spread to the kitchen.

Firefighters went to 14 Mansfeldt Road, Newbold, at around 1.20am after the family raised the alarm and escaped before the blaze spread to the house.

One fire crew fought the car fire while another used breathing apparatus to tackle the kitchen blaze.

The car was burned out and window frames, worktops and untensils in the kitchen were ruined. There was also smoke damage to the rest of the house.

Police say the cause of the fire is being treated as suspicious. Damage is estimated at around £7,000.

A newspaper cutting about the blaze from March 1995.

Chapter 6: Adam

Adam was born on Sunday afternoon on the 6th August 1995.

I started having pains early in the morning but I didn't want to go to hospital. I had a hot bath to try and ease the pain but it got worse.

Mum was at Nanna's house, helping with the cleaning, like she did every Sunday morning.

I got dressed and walked round to Nanna's. I can't believe I actually walked there, when I was in so much pain and about to give birth!

As soon as I got there, Mum took me back home and phoned the hospital to see if I could be admitted. They said yes. I remember sitting on the top of the stairs, telling my Mum that the pains had gone and I was okay. But my Mum didn't fall for it.

She drove me to hospital. I had to have another bath, and the midwives said that I was already half way through labour. I soon gave birth to Adam. Mum was there all the time with me.

I was scared that I wouldn't bond with him because throughout my pregnancy, I'd had nightmares and fears about giving birth to Gary's head on a baby's body. But I completely forgot about that when the baby was put into my arms.

Back then, you had to stay in hospital for three days after giving birth, especially with your first baby.

I kept asking the nurses to send me home. So after 24 hours, they let me, but only after a home inspection.

I was very protective of Adam, right from the start.

Looking back now, my sister, Sally, became more jealous at this time, if that was possible.

She thought Mum was fonder of Adam than of her kids. Mum treated them all the same. But Sally thought Mum was buying all of Adam's clothes and things. But she didn't. When Mum bought anything for Adam, she also bought something for Sally's kids. Plus, Mum had already given them lots of baby things when they were born and as they were growing up.

Sally was always trying to show me up or pull me down in front of other people. As I was now getting older and wiser, I started to realise what she was really like.

My brother, Jon, was like a brother to Adam. He was also very protective of him. But sometimes, he was a bit jealous of how Mum and Adam were together.

Jon and Adam would argue like brothers and wind each other up, but at the end of the day, they were very close. Adam looked up to Jon as a male role-model as he grew older.

Nanna spoilt Adam rotten, which was another thorn in my sister's side. But she didn't take into consideration that I took Nanna shopping every day. I helped Nanna and saw her every day. So did Adam. Sally was never there to help, not only my Nanna but anyone; she was selfish and only interested in herself. She was there for dinners out and parties but not for the hard work and helping out. But she expected to be treated the same as everyone who did help out.

When everything was okay with Sally, her family and her work place, we hardly saw her. We only saw her when she dropped her kids off or picked them up after babysitting for about eight hours, mostly longer, while she went to work.

The only other times when she would phone or visit were if she was having problems at work or if she found out that her husband was having another affair. As far as we know, he had a couple of affairs at work with his secretary – he moved jobs a few times. Sally always took him back, which he knew. It was like another of my Nanna's sayings: 'a leopard never changes his spots'.

I was still being stalked by Gary and I was desperately trying to make sure that it didn't affect Adam.

When we saw him in the street, I would try to avoid him, and if he caught me unawares, I would still ignore him and refuse to talk to him. Gary would be shouting and threatening me, intimidating me by yelling right up in my face. The only time I would speak to him was if he made a move towards Adam and threatened to take him away, and then I would shout at him to leave us alone.

This would happen quite often in the centre of town and looking back now, it upsets me to think that no one would come to our aid: a vulnerable young lady with a toddler being abused and threatened in a town full of people. What is the world coming to?

When Adam was really young, I would wait until Gary had gone, or had got both of us to somewhere safe. Then I would explain to Adam that the man had drunk too much alcohol and didn't know what he was doing or saying.

As Adam got older, and understood more, I did tell him that Gary was his father, but I still said that he shouted like that because he was drunk.

Adam never asked about his father but when he was about four, I had to start to tell him who his father was and that the reason we were not together was that we didn't get along. Also because Gary would stand in front of Adam's pushchair, shouting to him 'I'm your dad!'

When Adam got much older, he started to refuse to go to town or anywhere with me. Recently, I've begun to realise that it was probably because of the trauma that Gary caused to him with these incidents.

After one incident with his father, when he was older, I asked Adam if he wanted to see his father, but he quickly refused and didn't want to talk about it. Gary had scared him over the years with his behaviour towards me.

I never told Adam the bad things about his father. I wanted to protect him and allow him to make his own mind up when he was old enough to understand. I kept a folder with all the reports, newspaper clippings, letters and court papers to show Adam when he was older, so he could see that I was not making things up about his father and he could decide himself.

Adam had only one childhood and I didn't want to spoil it for him. It was difficult growing up as it was – all I could do was give him my love and support, like my Mum did for me.

I was still scared to go out alone. I only went to town for about an hour before the shops shut and then met Mum from work. She worked in the Co-op office in town. I knew that if I got into any trouble, I could walk to the Co-op, and most of the staff knew me because of Mum, so I felt safe there.

I was so stressed, unable to sleep and scared. I felt like a burden to my family and so guilty about all the trouble and problems I had bought to their door. My Mum, Dad and Nanna helped me the best they could, and I'm so eternally grateful for all their support.

I tried so hard to give Adam a normal upbringing and I'm surprised that he's turned out into a young man to be proud of.

He was always a happy-go-lucky kid and always had a big cheeky grin. People often commented on how well behaved and pleasant he was, especially when we went on coach holidays around the country. The other holiday makers would comment that they didn't realise there was a small child with them as he was so good.

I tried to give Adam all that I could. I think that maybe I felt guilty about him having no father, so I thought that I was trying to compensate for this by buying him toys, nice clothes and always being there for him as both a mother and father.

We were still living at my parents' house because I couldn't risk living on my own: I felt safe at my parent's.

With helping my Mum and seeing her bringing my brother up, I was a little wiser about dealing with Adam.

For example, such as dealing with temper tantrums and outbursts, my Mum would cook tea and my brother would say: 'I don't want that, I want something else!' So she would cook him something different, and then the following day, he'd ask for what Mum had cooked the day before!

I didn't do that with Adam. I just told him: 'you're having that or nothing.'

I can recall another incident from when my brother had just started driving and wanted a car with a big engine, but couldn't afford the insurance. I was standing in the doorway of the kitchen, my Mum was cooking and Jon was just going on and on about the car he wanted. He used to do this until Mum gave in.

He wanted my Mum to add the car onto her insurance policy. Mum was cooking boil in the bag fish, when all of a sudden, a frozen packet of cod in butter sauce hit the wall at the side of me, just missing my head. It all went quiet in the kitchen.

'I'm ever so sorry,' my Mum said. 'I was aiming at Jon, he's made me that het up!'

'You could have hit me!' my brother yelled.

'You're lucky it wasn't in the pan.' Mum said.

I was with Adam all the time up until he started school full time. The only time I was apart from him was when I had to go backwards and forwards to the courts for injunctions on Gary and also to act as a witness to Gary's previous criminal activities.

My Mum would always come along with me – good old Mum.

Nanna would look after Adam. I didn't trust anyone else to look after him, only Mum and Nanna.

Going backwards and forwards to the courts and trying to look after Adam and keep him safe was starting to take its toll on me.

I was in a taxi with Mum once, going to court about Gary, and I started physically shaking with nerves.

'I can't do it,' I said.

'Just do it, you know you can,' Mum said. 'He probably won't even turn up.' And he didn't.

Another time, I was in a small witness room at court and my Mum was with me as usual. Next thing I knew, Gary walked in. I was supposed to be in the witness room for my own protection. The court officials called the security guard to kick him out, but he just kept hanging around in the corridor outside the room, shouting and swearing so we could hear him. In the end, the court officials said we weren't needed anymore. I don't know what they told the jury.

Most of the time when I had to go to the courts about Gary, I was always told to leave early and taken through the back exits for my safety because Gary would kick off and cause trouble.

I was getting more and more stressed, anxious and also angry with the police, courts and the law system. It was just a big joke.

That was what life was like when Adam was a baby. Just courts and police. Having a baby is supposed to be a happy time, but it wasn't for me.

Eventually, I realised that it was just a waste of time and it was just a big game to Gary: he was enjoying it. He was getting the attention he craved from the police chasing him when we reported him, so we decided not to report anything he did unless it was a major thing where someone was hurt.

We ignored him and when we received letters from him, we filed them with the rest and we ignored his car driving up and down the street; the threats and taunts he shouted at us.

At last, after three long years of stalking and harassment, he calmed down, not altogether, but we started to have days and even months when we didn't see him. I was still nervous and on-edge, especially when I went out, as that now seemed to be a built-in instinct to me.

Gary's stalking may have subsided because he was busy elsewhere, as we discovered in the Derbyshire Times newspaper. Gary would often be in court or locked up for theft or drug charges. I think he was also more wary because of the new stalking and harassment laws being passed in parliament.

Another thing we found out was that Gary was a police informant. After the fire, we think Gary became an informant for the CID man we'd been dealing with, and he may have warned Gary off.

I was busy concentrating on Adam. I wanted him to have a good childhood like mine had been. As long as Gary kept away, everything was okay.

I don't think that anyone can understand what it's like to be stalked unless it's happened to them.

The feeling of having no control over your life – feeling helpless and scared all the time; jumping at every little noise; making sure everything is secure; always looking over your shoulder, worried for your family. Worrying *what he will do next – how far will he go?*

The feeling of avoiding crowded places because you can't see if he's there. Always going one way to a place and returning home a different way, in case he's following you. Only going to places where you know you're safe.

Never going out alone, especially in the dark. Having no real friends because you don't want to disrupt their lives and cause trouble for them – and because they don't understand what you are going through.

People say: 'ignore him, he'll get fed up and walk away', or imply that somehow you are doing things to encourage him. They think you make things up for attention, or don't believe you because you joke and smile, even though that's the only way you can cope with it.

Always being protective of family members, in case something happens to them. Feeling guilty for all the trouble that's happened and feeling that there is no way I can repay my family to say how sorry I am.

We kept getting reports from people about Gary. One was in February 1996. Someone told us that Gary was seen outside a house on Pennine Way, Loundsley Green, where his ex-girlfriend lived. Gary was sitting on a chair, wearing a balaclava and holding a shotgun. They said that the police and ambulance service had turned up but they didn't know what happened to him after that.

One incident occurred when the police were already at our house. Gary had broken his bail conditions and the police were just radioing through a warrant for his arrest. As they were doing this, Gary drove past in his lorry. The police were speechless.

The police were getting really annoyed and fed up with Gary. One officer asked us:

'Do you know anyone who could do him in?'

'If you found him dead in a gutter somewhere, who would you go to question about it'? I asked.

He replied: 'You.'

'Well, that's why he's still walking about.'

'As soon as we get a call through saying that Gary's dead, we'll throw a party at the police station', he said. The police were that fed up of him too!

It was also suggested that I go into a safe house. This would mean no contact with my family and living miles away, in a place I didn't know. It would be as if I was being punished for something that was not my fault. That was basically all the help and advice we got.

When Adam was fourteen months old in October 1997, he wasn't very well for the whole day. Late that evening, I was just putting him to bed when he went all limp and stopped breathing for a short time. We phoned for an ambulance and Adam was rushed into hospital. They kept him in overnight and I stayed with him. They diagnosed that Adam had suffered a febrile convulsion.

A febrile convulsion happens when a young child has a very high temperature, which then may cause them to have a seizure. This only lasts for a couple of minutes, but I can tell you, it is very scary and distressing thing to see. According to the doctors, it is a very common thing to happen in young children up to the age of three. In most cases, they never experience it again. Luckily, Adam never had another seizure.

In January 2000, Adam started school full-time at Newbold Church School. I picked this school for Adam to attend because it was in a more secure building than the other local schools at the time and I was still always thinking about his safety.

But before Adam started school, we had some terrible news.

Adam as a baby.

Even as a baby, Adam had a big, cheeky grin.

Adam with my Mum and Dad.

Adam with both his Nannas.

Chapter 7: A New Millennium

On Boxing Day 1999, my uncle Tony was taken into hospital with breathing problems. In the early hours of December 30th, we got a phone call from the hospital to say he had died. The whole family was devastated, especially my Nanna.

To see one of her children die before herself was traumatic for her. Tony had been ill for some time, but he'd never complained or said anything.

In the early 1990s, he'd had to sell his milk round, because in the early hours one morning, he was stopped by the police and given a breath test. He failed it because he had been drinking the night before, so he lost his licence. At the same time, he also had a blood test which showed that he was diabetic. After several more tests at the doctors, he found that he had Type 1 Diabetes, so he had to inject himself with insulin every day.

Also, after a routine diabetic check at the hospital, he was found to have a form of leukaemia but it was dormant and he was told that he didn't have to have treatment, but he did need to have regular check-ups at the hospital and tests on his bone marrow.

He also suffered from severe asthma and something called Dupuytren's contracture that made his fingers permanently clenched.

Tony was admitted to the hospital with breathing problems but according to the coroner's report, this then triggered his diabetes, which in turn started his leukaemia. It was all very technical and hard to understand.

We all missed Tony. As I've described before, he was a very lovable rogue, and everyone who knew him had some story to tell you about him.

His friends still visited my Nanna for years after he had died, because she always made everyone welcome and provided endless tea and coffee and sometimes sandwiches. She never had very much in the way of money and possessions, but what she did have, she would give or share with anyone.

It was hard to have to tell Adam that Tony had died. Adam had seen Tony every day when we went round to Nannas. The pair of them would always be tormenting one another.

In January 2000, a new millennium dawned and it started with Adam going to primary school and the funeral of my uncle Tony.

It was hard for me, because Adam had been with me for over four years, twenty-four-seven. Adam enjoyed going to school. He made new friends: his best friend was called Forest and I also became friends with his mum, Louise.

Adam mostly enjoyed the creative work at school. I did find that Adam was struggling with reading, but especially with writing.

I did try to make the teachers aware of this, but one parents evening, they brushed it off, saying: 'he's just a slow learner, give him time.' It wasn't just his writing. I noticed that he was copying letters and numbers back-to-front, but only certain ones.

Also, he was still finding it hard to tie his shoelaces and even to ride a bike. He was struggling with his balance and coordination. After reading up on it and getting Adam to do an online test, it showed that he was mildly dyslexic. I told the teachers again but once more, they fobbed me off with some story, as though I was just being over-cautious and didn't know what I was talking about.

Even today, Adam can't ride a bike and he's very clumsy.

While Adam was at school, I enrolled in adult education classes to try to get some qualifications to go back to work. I did sewing classes and a flower arranging course and I also studied counselling, psychology and health studies.

I was hoping to train as a counsellor, in the hope of helping similar people to me.

I also volunteered at the new Samaritans shop that had opened in town.

Around February 2003, we discovered a spot on the side of Adam's face.

The spot started to change from a small pea-size shape, growing bigger, changing shape and colour. We took him to the doctors, who referred him to a consultant at the hospital.

Within two weeks, he was booked in for an operation to have the tumour removed. It was a very worrying time, as you can imagine, with all sorts going through my head.

The doctors explained that because the tumour was positioned on the side of his face, it was near lots of nerves. Depending on how far down they had to cut to remove the entire tumour, the surgeons warned me that they might end up catching a nerve. There was a risk that Adam might wake up looking like he'd had a stroke. Luckily, the operation went well.

Adam was really good throughout all this and never complained. I was so proud of him.

We then had to wait another two weeks to find out the results. It was the longest two weeks you could have imagined, but eventually, we were told that everything was okay. The growth wasn't cancerous and he didn't need further treatment, but if he did get any more lumps, we were to go straight back to hospital.

Now Adam still has a faint scar on the side of his face.

Also in 2003, all of a sudden, the man who lived next door to us started to talk to me more, and every time I went out of the house, in the garden or looking through the window, he was there. I liked gardening and I only regularly left the house to take Adam to school and bring him home again. But the neighbour started to follow me when I went to fetch him and he was there outside, every time I was in the garden.

I couldn't understand it, as we had lived next door to him for over fifteen years. At first, I thought it was just coincidence but then I began to realise what he was doing. I ignored him, hoping he would get fed up and stop but he just got worse as the weeks went on.

He started making rude comments and suggestions when he saw me. He would be holding and rubbing himself down below as he spoke to me. He would stand in the window with no clothes on when I was in the garden, for me to see him.

It got so bad that I only left the house if I really had to, and I didn't tell anyone about the man's behaviour because I didn't want to cause trouble; he was married with three kids.

Eventually, after many months, I told my Mum because I was getting so stressed and scared. She knew there was something wrong, especially when one day, the neighbour replaced the fence in between our gardens with a much smaller one. My Mum went round and asked him what he was playing at.

He said that he was sorry and that he was going through a rough time at home with his wife and kids. But he still kept pestering me whenever he thought he could get away with it.

Eventually the neighbours moved house. Apparently, his wife found out that he had been calling chat lines and sleeping with prostitutes, so they split up.

2003 was an eventful year for another reason, because in August, the day after Adam's birthday, my brother got married to Beth. Jon had left school and done an apprenticeship in plumbing. After he qualified and worked for a company for a bit, he set up his own business.

He had been going out with Beth for a few years and they were renting their own place, but they still came round to Mum's every day for their tea or to get ready to go out into town most weekends.

Beth was from Holmegate in Clay Cross and Mum had heard the odd rumours about her, but she didn't say anything about it.

When Jon met Beth, she was working at a pub in town and then she worked at the local store in Holmegate. After a few months, we found out that she had to appear in court because the shop owners were charging her with theft. Apparently, she was on some fiddle or scam with the lottery scratch cards. A lot of money went missing. She appeared in court and was fined. This was only a couple of days before we were all going on holiday to Lanzarote. As you can imagine, it put the dampers on the holiday a bit.

Despite the theft, Jon still wanted to go ahead with the wedding. Jon and Beth asked if I would be one of their bridesmaids. I agreed at first, but as time went on,

I got really nervous and explained that I couldn't do it because I didn't feel comfortable standing up in public with a large group of people looking at me. My confidence was at a real low, and added stress wasn't helping. It was starting to make me physically ill.

My brother wasn't very pleased that I couldn't be a bridesmaid and he was upset, but after a while he was okay with me again. I think he understood eventually.

In return for his understanding, I made all the bouquets of flowers for the bride and bridesmaids, all the button holes, table and cake decorations and helped in any other way that I could.

The wedding was a big do and everyone looked like they were enjoying themselves.

Just before their first anniversary, Beth disappeared. We received a phone call from Jon saying she hadn't come home from work and he'd phoned her parents, family and friends and nobody had heard from her. We were all worried and tried to think where she could be. We even phoned the hospital and police station. Nothing.

Jon came to stay with us and it went on a few days, not knowing where she was. Then somehow, Jon began to realise that she had taken off with someone else. I don't know how he found out, but he started going out round town again and out drinking with his mates. But it was really because he was upset and maybe it was a way of getting back at her.

Jon stayed with us for a few months, until, all of a sudden, he came round and said he had heard from Beth and she wanted to meet him. Jon went to fetch her.

Apparently, she had met a bloke at work and went to stay with him, but now she wanted to return to Jon. They went away for a few days to discuss their relationship and when they came back, it was like nothing had happened. Beth's disappearance was never mentioned again. A short while later, Beth announced that she was pregnant.

Ashley was born in September 2005.

In February 2004, Grandad was taken ill and was admitted to hospital. He had been in a care home for a few years because he had dementia and kept falling over. He had been in and out of hospital a number of times, but this time, he deteriorated very fast and wasted away.

Towards the end, I couldn't visit him because I was upset about how he looked. I wanted to remember him as the man he was, my Grandad, not what he looked like at the end of his life.

Chapter 8: Holiday Antics

When we were kids, our summer holidays were always in Chapel St. Leonards and Ingoldmells, near Skegness.

We would always stay in a caravan with my Mum, Dad, Nanna, Grandad, sister and brother. Sometimes, well most of the time, my uncle Mike would turn up unexpectedly with one or two of his friends. When we were really young, we would be woken late at night with the caravan rocking and voices, one of which would be my Mum's, telling them to be quiet. In the morning, we would wake up to the smell of bacon and eggs and a room full of people.

We used to enjoy it – we had some good times.

The toilets were situated halfway down the caravan site, and my Grandad kept going up and down all night to go to the toilet, waking everyone up.

One holiday, my uncle and his friends decided to move the caravan steps. The next time Grandad went out to go to the toilet, he fell out of the caravan and all you could hear was a lot of stifled giggles. Grandad didn't get up in the night to "go" again after that.

Our holidays in this typical British seaside town would be spent walking along the seafront, playing on the amusements and sometimes at night, we would all go to the club on the caravan site.

When Adam was born, I would take him on coach holidays with my Mum, Dad and Jon. We went to Bournemouth, the Isle of Wight and Disneyland Paris.

We also all went abroad for the first time, to Lanzarote with my uncle Mike and his two kids. The following year, we went again and took my Nanna as well.

The age range on this holiday was from 6-80 years old. It was a holiday to remember.

Right at the start, we got into trouble, as we were going through the scanner in the airport. Nanna turned to my Mum and said, as a joke: 'are you going to tell them where you've hidden your gun, Jean?'

The next thing we knew, armed police and security were standing next to us.

Of course, my Mum was searched but we were laughing, watching the scenario unfold. My uncle kept apologising to the airport staff, saying that my Nanna was old, didn't know what she was saying and she had never been abroad before.

My poor Mum was terrified and we were given a lecture on the seriousness of saying things like that by the airport staff.

This was only a few months after the 9/11 disaster.

Coming back through customs at the airport, we were stopped yet again. Because we flew back to Britain on a late flight, we were all tired and just wanted to get home, so we had thrown all our suitcases on trolleys and proceeded to go through customs.

Jon and Beth got split up from the group as it was busy. The officers stopped them because they were pushing a trolley with three suitcases on and there were only two of them. They were taken to one side as the rest of us went through the barriers without a problem. The next thing we knew was that they were asking for my Mum to go back through and answer some questions.

Mum was carrying all our passports and keeping them safe so we didn't lose them. When Jon and Beth were asked routine questions such as: 'Is this your suitcase?' 'Have you packed it yourself?' and 'Has anyone tampered with it?' Jon's answers weren't what the officers expected.

'No, these aren't our suitcases and we haven't packed them.' Jon said. 'And my Mum's got my passport.'

Again, we were given another telling off and a lecture about why it's important to carry your own case and your own passport, even if you are part of a big family travelling together.

We were glad to get back home!

Chapter 9: My Best Friends

In March 2006, my Nanna passed away. She had been ill for a few months before she died. She had started to lose her memory and forget things.

She was staying at our house because she wasn't safe to be on her own.

Over the past few months, I noticed that she was still in bed or wasn't ready when I picked her up to take her shopping. We began to realise that she was getting mixed up with her times and seemed confused about whether it was morning or night.

Once I went round and a friend of my uncle Tony's was sitting there with a cup of coffee and a plate of sandwiches. My Nanna was out of sorts and she took me into the kitchen.

'I don't know who that man is,' she said.

At first, I thought she was joking, and then realised that she was worried and serious.

'Who do you think he is?' I asked. 'You've just made him a sandwich and a drink.'

'He said he was a friend of Tony's, so I let him in.'

I explained to her that it was Arthur, a friend of my late uncle's. I reminded Nanna that we'd known him for years and that he visited her quite often.

She just laughed it off.

'That's okay then,' she said. 'Maybe I'm not safe on my own,' Nanna added jokingly.

But she was right. I tried to tell her that in future, she shouldn't let anyone into her house if she didn't know them and to keep her door locked, but I knew my words were falling on deaf ears. I guess it was hard for her to change her caring and helpful ways after all those years, even if she needed to be more wary to take better care of herself.

It also didn't help my Nanna much that my uncle Mike had brought my Nanna's council house dirt-cheap because she had lived there for over fifty years and he was now divorced and living in a flat on his own. Mike conned Nanna into letting him buy the house and moving in.

Not satisfied with that, he started to knock the house to bits, altering the bathroom and kitchen. Sometimes, Nanna was left on her own all day without any water or heating. I would go round to find that she had bottles of water saved for when she wanted a wash or drink.

It didn't matter to Mike because he was out at work all day and lived on takeaway food.

I started having my dinners with Nanna at midday, after we'd been shopping. Usually I had my main meal of the day after five o'clock, when everyone was home from work and school.

I would bring Nanna round to our house and make us both something to eat and then take her home again. This was also a way to make sure she was eating properly. She was still stubborn and independent, so it was a way to look after her, yet let her have some form of control.

Nanna did start to deteriorate more, and in the end, she came to live at our house because she had also started to fall.

One night, in the early hours of the morning, we found her struggling to breathe. We phoned for an ambulance and she was taken into hospital. She died later that day. The doctors explained that she had been suffering with an enlarged heart.

I was shocked, devastated and lost without her. She was a second mum to me.

Adam was also upset, as Nanna used to spoil him rotten, and they thought the world of one another.

Then in August, my Mum went to work as normal in the morning but as she was going to work, she didn't feel too well; she had a pain in her chest.

When she got to work, she saw the first aider there, who said it was probably indigestion and sent her home for the day.

Mum had tried to phone me so I could come and fetch her, but I didn't hear the phone because I was cleaning up and hoovering, so she caught the bus home. Mum came into the house and explained that she was having chest pains.

I rang the doctors and made an appointment for Mum. It had just gone 9am at this point, and the appointment was for about 10.30am.

Mum went upstairs, to lie on her bed. I carried on with the housework and got Adam ready as he was still in his pyjamas.

I could hear Mum go into the bathroom; she was being sick. I took a glass of water upstairs for her and Mum lay back down on the bed. I asked if she was ok and put the water on the bedside table. Then I went back downstairs to finish getting Adam ready and also to take our dog, Ellie on the garden.

As I reached the bottom of the stairs, I heard a strange noise. I ran upstairs to see Mum in a bad way, struggling to breathe and her lips were going blue. I quickly phoned for an ambulance and passed the phone to Adam, who stayed on the phone with the emergency operator while I tried chest compressions on Mum until the paramedics came to take over.

I stayed upstairs with them and saw that they tried to resuscitate her several times. After what seemed like hours, they told me to go downstairs.

In the kitchen, Adam had been phoning members of the family to tell them that Mum had been taken very ill, and Jon arrived straight away. He was devastated, as he was very close to Mum. I explained what had happened. The paramedics told us to wait in the kitchen while they put Mum in the ambulance, and then we followed the ambulance to the hospital.

When we arrived at the hospital, they took us into a side room in the A&E department. Jon went to meet other members of the family and his wife outside the hospital, to show them where we were.

After a short time, a doctor and nurse came into the room and told me and Adam that they were very sorry, but Mum had died. Just as we'd been told this terrible news, my Dad, sister and brother walked in.

We were all crying, completely devastated. We couldn't believe it; we were all in shock. It was like some kind of nightmare; it didn't seem real.

My sister Sally visited Mum every day while she lay in the chapel of rest. It was a shame that she hadn't visited my Mum as often as that when she was alive.

I think Sally was feeling guilty, because she knew deep-down that she should have been there more for Mum.

I had always bought Mum and Nanna flowers, every week. There was a regular "buy one bunch, get one free" offer at the supermarket. We would joke about whose bunch was free that week.

I did it to show how much I appreciated them and so that they could benefit from the beauty of the flowers while they were alive.

Everything was a blur – the funeral arrangements and everyday life carrying on without Mum.

All I can remember from the funeral was that the crematorium was packed out with Mum's friends, family and work colleagues. That was a lovely surprise and I felt humbled to see how many lives Mum had touched.

Lots of Co-op staff were there to pay their respects. In fact, we were told afterwards that the Co-op had to recruit staff from other shops to cover for them for the morning of Mum's funeral.

A few weeks after the funeral, my sister kept on at me about sorting Mum's stuff out and I told her we would do it when Dad was ready.

After a few months, Dad asked if I would sort out my Mum's clothes and things, because he didn't want my sister to do it. He said: 'you know what she's like and I can't be doing with it.'

In other words, she was a bit of a drama queen and it was upsetting enough for Dad, without Sally blubbering and getting hysterical.

I agreed and I cleared out the wardrobes to give my Mum's things to charity. My Dad asked family members if anyone wanted anything that had belonged to Mum.

Of course, Sally piped up. She wanted Mum's wedding ring and some other jewellery. She also went through the bags of clothes before we donated them and was annoyed that I had sorted them out myself.

'Why didn't you tell me?' she snapped.

My Dad usually stayed out of arguments between us, but he told Sally that he'd asked me to do it.

I had also sorted out some of my clothes too, and put them in the bags with Mum's clothes for the charity shop.

Sally took out a jumper and a cardigan, which were actually both mine!

'Can I take these?' she asked.

'Yes of course,' I said. I didn't have the heart to tell her they were mine. That's how much Sally knew my Mum – she didn't even know what clothes she wore.

'Are you sure I can have them?' she asked, crying into my old cardie.

She wanted them to remind her of Mum!

Sally was given Mum's wedding ring and Dad gave me Mum's eternity ring.

A few years previously, Mum had been diagnosed with thyroid problems, and one of the symptoms was her fingers swelling up, so her rings became too tight for her.

Dad brought her new rings that fitted her. Mum gave me her original engagement and wedding rings.

'I want to know that you've got them,' she said. 'Because I know that if anything happened to me, you'd end up with nothing because you'd just let the others have all the stuff – and you wouldn't say anything.'

How right she was.

This was something else that my sister didn't know about my Mum.

Every time I saw Sally afterwards, she kept saying: 'you don't mind me having Mum's wedding ring, do you?'

'No, of course not,' I kept saying, because I had the rings Mum had already given to me.

But Sally still kept on at me. In the end, she got on my nerves so much that I told her about Mum giving me her original rings years ago – Sally wasn't best pleased!

After a while, I asked Dad if I could have my Nana's wedding ring, which Mum had saved when she died. He said yes and gave it to me.

I didn't want my sister to have it and I didn't feel guilty about it, because as far as I was concerned, I did more for my Nanna than Sally ever did.

Mum did everything for everybody, so somehow, automatically, her responsibilities ended up with me. I didn't have time to grieve properly. My Dad was devastated, so I tried to make things alright for him.

Mum used to sort out and pay all the household bills, and Dad asked me to take over her role of sorting out the family's finances, so I had to make sure that everything was paid. I had to do all the shopping and cooking, and do anything else that the family wanted.

My brother kept coming round, and also my uncle and his kids, which was understandable, but I spent all my time making cups of tea and having to make everybody's dinners, so it just felt like I was becoming my Mum, rather than having time to grieve for her. I didn't want any of these responsibilities – it was just assumed that I would take them on.

I'd also got Adam to care for too. I didn't really have time to sit down and talk to him properly.

I never really had time to grieve for two of the most important people in my life.

I also feel guilty about my Mum's death because I feel like I should have gone upstairs sooner. Maybe I could have done more to save her. I still feel guilty that she tried to call me for a lift and then had to take the bus. But that's life, I suppose. I was vacuuming and couldn't hear the phone. Even the first aider hadn't spotted that my Mum was showing signs of an impending heart attack.

I know that certain members of my family have blamed me for Mum's death; even though they have not actually said it, it's been implied.

Maybe it was time for my Mum to go, as according to another of my Nanna's sayings, 'when your time is up and your number is called, there's nothing you can do about it'.

My two best friends: Mum and Nanna.

Chapter 10: Life Goes On

Mum's funeral was held the same week that Adam started at Newbold Community Secondary School.

It felt like déjà-vu, as uncle Tony's funeral had been held when Adam started at primary school.

Adam's school was just down the road from us. He didn't like it there because his best friend Forest was going to a different school and Adam found it hard to make new friends. He started to fall behind with his schoolwork. I think that the death of his grandmother and great-grandmother within a short period of time didn't help, and he missed them too.

I was struggling to cope and I guess that I was also too busy trying to keep the house tidy, pay the bills for Dad, cooking, washing, ironing and also, I was baby-sitting a lot, looking after my nephew Ashley.

Just before Mum died, my brother had bought a house two doors down from my parents', and he had moved in a few weeks after she passed away.

So it was convenient to keep dropping Ashley off for me to look after.

At one point, a neighbour said: 'I thought he was yours as you've got him all the time.'

I was struggling. I was missing my Mum and Nanna and I regret that I didn't have enough time to spend with Adam like I'd done previously. Also, I was feeling guilty that I hadn't done enough to save Mum.

Plus, I was working as a volunteer at a charity shop on Newbold road. That was to try to get me out of the house and back in to work.

After Mum and Nanna died, I struggled to go out. Whenever I did, people would ask where my Mum or Nanna were, because I had always been out with one or both of them.

Gary found out that I was working in the charity shop and kept coming in and asking for me and leaving me cards and letters.

Gary also started to come round to our house again, demanding to see Adam, but Adam didn't want to see him.

Finally, I showed Adam the folder I had been keeping for him, with evidence of the things Gary had done to me.

'I didn't want to tell you while you were still young,' I said. But because Gary was demanding to see him and Adam was old enough to understand, I told him he could read the folder if he wanted to. 'Just so you know that I'm not lying to you – all the official papers are in there, from the courts and solicitors. So you know it's true.'

I left Adam with the folder to read in his own time.

He came downstairs later on, upset.

'I'm sorry,' he said. 'I thought that when everyone was talking about the fire, it was a chip pan fire.' He hadn't realised that his father had deliberately caused the fire.

We had tried to not discuss the fire in front of Adam, but when my sister came round, we would have to watch what she said in front of him. Sally always wanted to poke her nose in and get involved; she liked the drama of things, but then she would go home and leave everyone with all the baggage and mess to deal with afterwards.

As Adam got older, he became terrified of turning out like his father – and he still is scared that he might be like him. He's frightened that he's inherited "bad genes" from Gary.

If anyone tells Adam that he's just like his dad, it really upsets him. It's the worst thing you can say to him.

One day, Adam said to me, 'You must hate me.'

'Why?'

'Because I look like him.'

'You do – of course you're going to – but you're nothing like him. You just make a go of yourself, get a job and do well. Because that's nothing like your dad, and if he knew that, it would hurt him more than anything.'

Adam made me proud. He's acted very grown up and mature about Gary. He still doesn't want to see his father, even when I tell him it's okay, as long as he takes someone with him and he isn't on his own with him.

In October 2008, I started working for a cleaning company called Molly Maid. It was only supposed to be part-time but I ended up working full-time. I enjoyed it, and it was ideal for me because I was travelling to different places and wasn't in one place all the time. We would clean private houses, pubs, factories, offices, holiday houses and stately homes.

The job helped me to regain my confidence gradually, meeting all sorts of people. Every day was different (but that's another story).

Being busy at work was another reason why I didn't notice that Adam was having problems at school. In 2009, I eventually found out that he was skiving school – and it was because he was being bullied.

Eventually, I also found out that the reason he was being bullied was because he was gay.

Adam was moody and his behaviour was not normal. I was worried that he was on drugs, and Jon and I searched Adam's room together.

Searching Adam's bedroom was a bit like a Bear Grylls expedition, which is something you'll know if you have any teenage children!

We found a notebook that Adam's teachers had asked him to write in because of the bullying, to help him to express his thoughts and feelings.

Jon and I later confronted Adam about the notebook and also apologised to him about searching his room, but explained that we'd felt so worried about him, we had needed to do it.

Adam was upset and started to cry. He said that he couldn't tell us about being gay because he was frightened that nobody would love him and we would have nothing to do with him anymore.

I told him it didn't matter if he was straight or gay, he was still my son and I would always love him, no matter what. I told Adam I would support him in whatever path he chose in life, as long as he was happy.

After a few more months, I moved Adam from Newbold School to Parkside School, and I noticed a big improvement with his attitude and his school work.

But later this year, I took another overdose of tablets. Everything was getting too much for me. I felt guilty about Adam being bullied and how he didn't feel that he could tell me about it. But in a way, I understood why, as I had been in a similar situation when I was young. But it hurt me to know that he was going through it alone.

I was also still missing my Mum and Nanna. I had no one to turn to and no one to talk to.

Not only was I working full-time, cleaning four or five places a day, but I was also cooking, cleaning, doing all the household chores in the week and shopping and babysitting at the weekends. Not just for Ashley, but now he had a baby sister called Samantha.

In 2010, Adam discovered a lump on his private parts. The doctor referred him to the hospital for a scan. The scan showed that the lump was nothing to worry about; it was a cyst.

However, from the scan, they found that he had testicular microlithiasis, which is a relatively common condition, only diagnosed by ultrasound scan, in which small clusters of calcium form in the testicles. A number of studies show an increased risk of testicular cancer and infertility for men with this condition.

Going through this with Adam was upsetting and I worried for months, but so far, everything is fine.

In 2011, Adam left school and started an apprenticeship to become an electrician. Growing up, he had always wanted to be a doctor or a nurse.

But I think my brother talked him into doing the electrician course, because when Adam became qualified, he could use him for jobs he needed at his work.

I was still working hard and trying to cope with everyone, as family members still came to me when they needed anything.

I was having a few issues at work. The woman I had first started working with was great fun, and we would have a laugh at work together. However, she started going out with a man she'd met and their relationship didn't seem to be going well. She was always stressed, crying and forever texting or phoning her boyfriend while she was at work.

She was having trouble paying her rent so I lent her some money. She agreed to pay me back each week when we got our wages, until it was all paid back. Everything was okay for the first few weeks; then she stopped paying me.

I asked her what was happening, and she promised she would pay me back the following week.

The next thing I knew, she was buying £70 trainers for her boyfriend and paying for other stuff that wasn't really essential. She had also found that she was pregnant and was planning a big wedding abroad.

I was angry with her and asked her to pay my money back. She got upset and said that I was picking on her and that we were supposed to be friends.

She sent the money to me, but our friendship was no more. She left work not long after that. I was upset. I felt let down again by another so-called friend; it was like school all over again. This was what had hurt me the most.

I was made route manager at work: this meant that I was given a work car which I had to look after, and I would drive round to all the jobs. We would have to work in pairs, sometimes in a three. The other cleaners were called assistants.

I was given another lady to work with. She was older than me but she didn't do much work and when she did do anything, she did it wrong.

We had to keep returning to jobs to put things right. I was literally doing the work of two people. I was getting exhausted and was very stressed.

Eventually, she left and I ended up with another assistant called Rosie, who was in her early twenties. I already knew Rosie and her family a little, because they lived next door to my Nanna's house.

At the end of 2013, I was involved in a car accident whilst driving at work. It wasn't my fault – the other car involved in the accident drove into the side of our car because she was going too fast and wasn't paying attention.

She admitted liability but it didn't stop me from feeling guilty because it was the work car. Thankfully, my boss was okay about it and was more concerned for mine and Rosie's welfare.

I ended up with torn muscles in my shoulder and back and lots of bruises. I had to take two weeks off work.

In November of this year, my Dad had to go into hospital in Sheffield to have one of his kidneys removed. Adam and I took him to the hospital in the morning and I returned to the ward later with my brother, to visit Dad after his operation.

We visited Dad for the next few days. I would either book a taxi or catch the bus to get to Sheffield. It took a full day trip to go and visit him.

When Dad returned home, I had to care for him. My sister had visited Dad every day in the hospital, but soon as he came back home, she only visited him on odd occasions.

I found that this was often the case with Sally. If any family members were in hospital, you would see her all the time. I think she liked the drama and attention of hospitals, and because she was a First Aid trainer, she thought that she was as medically trained as a doctor or nurse.

This was embarrassing, because Sally would come out with all these technical medical terms to the hospital staff, as though she was telling them how to do their jobs. You could tell what they thought of her "expert knowledge" by the looks on their faces.

Dad made a good recovery, but he also played on the attention he was getting.

Chapter 11: When Will It Ever End?

2014 was another busy, traumatic year. I had been chatting online to someone from the Czech Republic. It was on a site for pen pals, and he wanted to learn English.

As we got chatting and talking more, he invited me over to visit. So in May, I arranged to go over and I had a really nice time. When I arrived back home, we still kept in touch and not only was I teaching him English, but I had started to learn the Czech language. We had arranged that he was going to visit me at the end of the year and I arranged to visit again, later in July.

But suddenly, he started making excuses and saying that he was too busy to talk to me. Then I found out that he had used me and I was only a friend to him, nothing else.

While I was away, he had taken me to meet his parents and was talking as though we were a couple. He was even looking for jobs for me there. I had also slept with him, and I suspected I was now pregnant. I was being sick all the time and had missed my period.

I cancelled my visit to him in July, only a couple of days before I was due to fly to the Czech Republic.

I felt stupid and angry, not only with him but with myself for being so stupid. I had already started self-harming again, but this time, it was worse. Every day, I was also taking tablets, and increasing the amount each day.

Everything was spiralling out of control.

My brother and sister-in-law found out that I had taken all those pills, and Beth took me to hospital, where I was admitted. The hospital staff said that because it was a staggered overdose, I had to stay on a drip to counteract the tablets I had taken.

While the nurse went through the routine questions, one of the questions was: 'Did I self-harm?' This was the first time in my life that anyone had asked me that. I looked at the nurse, then looked at Beth and just said quietly, 'yes'.

The nurse then continued asking questions, but I could feel Beth's eyes burning into me. I felt ashamed and embarrassed. This was the first time that anybody was aware that I self-harmed. It wasn't my secret anymore.

It was hard for my family to understand my self-harm. I couldn't explain why I did it in a way that could help them to understand what it was like for me.

It's like an addiction once I start doing it, like taking the tablets. Then I get scared I will go too far. But at the beginning, it makes me feel like I have some control over my life and I can control the pain and hurt I'm feeling.

But when I explained it that way, my family looked at me with hurt and confusion and that made me feel like I was an alien from another planet. I know it's wrong, but at the time it gave me control and a sort of release for my emotions.

After coming out of hospital, I was offered counselling. I went to the same NHS mental health service on St. Mary's Gate where I'd been all those years ago as a teenager.

I will call the counsellor who was assigned to me Michael. I was given appointments every week, and sometimes, it would be a home visit.

The counsellor also started to text me more often on his work phone and then one day, he said that his work phone's battery was running low and so he started to text me on his own personal phone. His visits became more frequent.

I trusted him and agreed to meet him secretly, as he said that no one could know about us: he would lose his job. He told me that in another three years, he would be taking early retirement and then it wouldn't matter.

I was stupid and naive enough to believe him. He started to want me to meet him at weekends and at night times in car parks.

He was getting friendlier: kissing, fondling and touching me, and he seemed to be acting more aggressively, not tender and kind. I can remember him trying to undo my trousers but I stopped him. It was going too fast for me.

Then, in November, I started taking too many tablets again and was having severe stomach cramps and being sick. I texted Michael and told him about it and said I was sorry but I was misusing tablets again.

Michael texted back to say that he couldn't cope with someone dying on him again and that he couldn't deal with it. I was asking for help but he ignored me.

Near Christmas time, he started to make excuses that he wasn't very well and then, over the Christmas holidays, I only had one text from him, to say that he was ill. I didn't hear anything else from him.

I knew that he wasn't ill over the Christmas holidays because he was still going to the pub and to football matches and was still working.

Until Christmas, he'd been texting me all day, every day. But in the New Year, he started to act all professional again, as though nothing had ever happened between us.

He had been cancelling our counselling appointments, but then one day, out of the blue, he texted me about booking an appointment.

I didn't reply straight away, as I was feeling confused, upset and ill. I was struggling to cope again.

When I did text him back about the message, to make an appointment to see him in January, he replied to say that he couldn't make an appointment anyway, because he was feeling under the weather and was going home early.

I didn't get in touch with him to make another appointment. I blocked his personal number but not his work mobile number. He didn't get in touch professionally either as my support worker. In other words, he left me to struggle on my own, with no help.

I think the reason why he stopped wanting to see me and started to make excuses was because I'd told him I was falling for him, to which he replied that he couldn't have people falling for him.

It was then that I began to realise that I had been used and that I deserved something better than a quick grope in the back of a car.

Several times, I asked him why he'd chosen me. He said that it just happened and what we had was special.

I discovered that it was one big lie.

I hated myself for being so weak and pathetic. I was beginning to wonder why all this stuff was happening to me. Was it because I was a bad person? What was I doing wrong? It was getting harder each time to pick myself up and face the next challenge.

I was running out of energy and hope.

Chapter 12: Voldemort

Back in July 2014, I picked up a leaflet from the library about a self-help group called the Butterfly Project. They met each Wednesday at a community centre in Chesterfield. I plucked up enough courage to go, and I'm so glad that I did.

The group I found there were really helpful and helped me to understand the reasons why I wanted to harm myself. I learned how to handle my feelings, and how to use coping strategies instead of self-harm.

It was a relief to know that there were others who knew exactly how I was feeling, without needing to explain everything. The Butterfly Project group was supportive, helpful and like a family. We were from all walks of life, all different, but united by one thing: self-harm.

I had started to accept the fact that I was a self-harmer but my family were still finding it hard to understand. I'd even had a few comments saying I was just doing it for attention. If I was just doing it for attention, why hadn't I told anyone all those years ago when I'd started to self-harm at school?

The Butterfly Project was a group which taught you how to cope using different methods, such as mindfulness, and to find what worked best for each individual.

We also played games, had movie nights, pizza nights, and went on outings.

The annual Butterfly Project outing to the Dogs Unleashed show at Bakewell is still going strong.

Another outing I joined them for was walking and climbing in Edale. We climbed up Jacob's Ladder to Kinder Scout.

It was a bonding time for the group, as everyone helped each other climb up to the highest point in the Peak District. It was a great sense of achievement to reach the top, and we ate our sarnies on our special picnic rock. It proved that we could achieve what looked impossible, with a little help and encouragement from friends.

In a session at one of the Butterfly meetings, back in February 2015, I described what had happened between me and Michael. I told them I was upset and confused because I didn't understand what I had done wrong.

The two leaders of the group looked at one another, and then they called a break and asked if they could talk to me outside.

They asked me exactly what had happened with Michael. They both were shocked, and explained to me that what he had done was illegal and was against all the codes of practice of a mental health nurse. He was in serious trouble. They carried on and explained that what had happened was not my fault; I was the victim and was vulnerable. Even though I was an adult, he should have known better. In legal terms, what he'd done was similar to a teacher grooming a child and sexually exploiting them.

I told them that he didn't force me, but they said it still didn't matter. He was responsible for my welfare and safety; he was a trained, qualified professional nurse. What he'd done was not allowed.

I was asked if I had been receiving any counselling or other support since he stopped contact.

'No,' I replied. 'I've not heard anything from him or the centre for a few weeks.'

The group leaders were appalled and disgusted and said that he was in serious trouble. They said that I needed to talk to one of the co-founders of the Butterfly Project group, called Gina.

They arranged a meeting for me with her the following week.

When I met her, I told her what I had told the others. She was also disgusted and shocked that a fellow colleague in a similar profession to herself could do this.

She immediately started to arrange for me to go on an emergency safeguarding procedure, and with my consent, wrote out a statement to report Michael for what had happened during the last few months. This was reported to the Derbyshire Health Care Trust and also the police.

He was reported for sexual abuse and psychological neglect and misconduct.

Michael was suspended with immediate effect and pending further investigation.

Everything seemed to be happening all at once. It was hard trying to process it all and it took a long time for me to understand what was wrong. I didn't want people getting into trouble and losing their jobs and friends. I knew what kind of ripple effect it would have.

I was asked to attend several meetings over the following months, by the safeguarding people, the Manager of Healthcare at St. Mary's Gate (Michael's boss) and the people from the NHS trust who were investigating the case.

At all the meetings I attended, Gina was there by my side, giving me lots of support and explaining what each meeting was about. She was determined to fight my corner. I can't thank her enough for being there with me.

Gina and the Butterfly Project were really nice to me and kept asking if I was okay. I just said 'yes'.

But the truth was, I was still confused, and felt guilty, upset and embarrassed.

It was decided that I needed to go to another counsellor. Gina referred me to a counsellor and said that she was really good and the best at her job. The only trouble was that I had to travel to Killamarsh every week to see her, which was about thirty minutes' drive away.

I was upset because at one point, I felt that I was being punished because I had to go out of Chesterfield to see the counsellor. I wasn't allowed to see anyone in Chesterfield because they all knew Michael and his fellow colleagues. The people handling my case said that they didn't want the other counsellors to know about Michael, because it would be upsetting for them and would break confidentiality for him.

Supposedly, only a handful of people knew about the situation.

In fact, Gina came up with the nickname for Michael: Voldemort – *He-Who-Must-Not-Be-Named.*

In January 2016, I had the last meeting with the NHS Trust team investigating my case. They explained that they couldn't tell me too much because of protecting Michael's privacy. But they told me that he was no longer working for the NHS and would never work for them in the future.

It had taken them nearly a year to investigate my case and they apologised for the delay, but they explained that when they started looking into Michael's work history and investigated his phone records, they kept finding more and more things that they needed to check. Michael had been working for them for many years, so there was a lot to check.

They wouldn't tell me what they had found; only that it wasn't very good. However, they explained that they had dealt with or were still dealing with the issues they had discovered.

I asked if Michael had done this to anyone else. They replied that they couldn't comment but not to worry, things were being dealt with. They also informed me that if Michael ever applied for a job involving children, the elderly or the vulnerable, it would be flagged up on his DBS record, to inform his future employer to check up on him.

I was worried about him doing something similar to someone else. Maybe now, looking back, it was because I felt guilty that I didn't report the man who raped me when I was younger and was still carrying the guilt that I could have protected others.

This time I could do something about it.

I later found out from a reliable source that Michael had taken advantage of at least six other women.

I was also told that it was a long process because the Derbyshire Health Trust hadn't really dealt with anything like this before, so they were having to learn about what to do and put future plans and procedures in place so that it never happened again.

They apologised for what Michael had done and thanked me and said that they were really grateful to me for coming forward and reporting him. They appreciated that it was very difficult for me, especially with my previous problems, and now he had added to them.

The Derbyshire Health Trust said I was very brave, but I didn't really feel like that. I just wanted to make sure that he didn't abuse anybody else again for his sick, perverted pleasure.

I somehow still felt that it was my fault; that I was being punished yet again for something that was entirely my fault. I had caused all this chaos and extra work for everyone. I felt like an embarrassment and a nuisance to everyone.

And sometimes, it felt like they were protecting Michael and trying to cover up what had happened. They just kept talking about his privacy and confidentiality. But what about mine?

They had downloaded my messages and information from my mobile phone; they had been through every little detail in my medical records, and I was even put through the pain of having psychiatric assessments by independent doctors. This was painful and depressing for me, because it brought up all the past events I had experienced.

When the investigation was nearly finished, someone told me to make a claim for the damage and upset that Michael had caused. They gave me some leaflets to read.

I didn't think any more about it, but some weeks later, I picked them up and read them. I started to make enquires and ended up getting in touch with a firm of solicitors based in Essex.

I didn't trust any solicitors in Chesterfield and I thought I stood a better chance with a company further afield, plus they specialised in medical and abuse cases.

This proved a good move, but it took my solicitor nearly three years to get a result.

At first, the NHS trust would not reply to any of my letters or calls, and then, when they eventually acknowledged them, they would keep stalling and asking for different types of information and my medical records. It looked like the case was to going to court, but suddenly, they informed my solicitor that they were prepared to settle out of court.

I attended a further assessment with another doctor. I also received a letter of apology via the solicitor saying they were sorry for the behaviour of their employer. Which, according to the solicitor, is very rare.

After nearly four years of re-living the pain and hurt of the past, and being embarrassed and ashamed by retelling the events, I was paid a very large sum in compensation.

The first thing I did was to make a big donation to the Butterfly Project group who were a big help and support to me, so they can keep up the good work and help other people dealing with self-harm.

The Butterfly Project conquers Kinder Scout!

NHS
Derbyshire Healthcare
NHS Foundation Trust

Your Ref:

Directors Suite
Trust Headquarters
Ashbourne Centre
Kingsway Site
Kingsway
DERBY
DE22 3LZ

12 July 2018

Strictly Private and Confidential

Dear Mrs Brough

I write to you as the Chief Executive of Derbyshire Healthcare NHS Foundation Trust.

On behalf of the Trust, I would like to offer my sincere apology for the failings in the care afforded to you during your treatment around November 2014 to January 2015. I am sure that this was an extremely upsetting time for you and I am very sorry to hear of the distress that this has caused you.

I would like to personally thank you for coming forward. I am most grateful for your assistance and co-operation with the investigation. I appreciate that this must have been difficult for you.

I understand the lawyers for the Trust will be working towards resolving your claim and I hope this will help you to secure some resolution.

I hope you can accept this apology and I would like to wish you well for the future.

Yours sincerely

Chief Executive

Trust Headquarters, Ashbourne Centre, Kingsway Hospital, Derby DE22 3LZ

The apology letter that the NHS finally sent to me.

Chapter 13: Paul

In July 2015, I started to talk to Paul on an internet chat site. We agreed to meet in the town centre outside the old BHS store on Vicar Lane.

Paul said he was coming straight from work and he was standing there as promised, waiting outside the shop. He looked even more nervous than me. He was dressed in his work uniform; he worked as a patient services assistant at the Chesterfield Royal hospital in Calow.

After introductions, we went to the BHS café and had a coffee. From the start, we got on really well. It felt like I had already known him for a long time. We agreed to meet the following day and since that day in July, we have never looked back.

In fact, we got on so well that on the 25th August 2015, we got engaged. This was also the day when we moved into our flat together. And on the 29th February 2016, we got married.

I explained to Paul what had happened to me in the past, so there were no secrets between us. I thought it was best. Paul was okay about it and is very supportive and understanding.

We've been together for four years now and it's not been plain sailing. We have had a few problems, starting with my family.

I introduced Paul to my Dad, Adam, Jon and Beth within a few days of meeting him. Everyone got on okay with him and it looked as if my luck was changing at last.

Everything was fine until the time I said that we were looking for a flat together. Jon came round to Dad's house on the day that we had brought Tiger, Paul's Staffie, to meet my dogs: Ellie the Westie, and the two pugs Tio and Oscar.

Tiger was a rescue dog. Paul had recently got him from the RSPCA kennels and he was very nervous and didn't like loud noises or shouting. So when my brother came round and started shouting and arguing, Paul took Tiger outside because the dog was stressed.

I can't really remember what the argument was about or how it started, but Jon came round shouting at Adam. He kept on and on and said some horrible, nasty things to me and Adam; things that still hurt me to this day.

Jon also kicked off about me moving out and getting married. I can understand that maybe he was concerned about me jumping into things too fast, but he went the wrong way about it.

I thought that Jon would be happy for me, but now, looking back at the situation, perhaps he was angry because I wasn't going to be at the family's beck and call any more and they wouldn't be able to control me.

As before, my family were always asking where or what I was doing and where I had been.

My Dad told me to ignore Jon and told me that as long as I was happy and Paul was treating me okay, that was all that mattered. He said that Jon would come round to my marriage in the end.

In September, Paul and Adam and I moved into our flat at Wyedale Court, Littlemoor. It was only a ten-minute walk down the road from Dad, and we told him he could visit us at any time.

Jon had been in touch and wanted us all to go out for a meal to discuss our wedding plans. We had set a date for 29th February the following year.

It was a bit uncomfortable at first as things had been tense between me and Jon, but then we relaxed and it seemed like things were returning to how they used to be.

But then, when the wedding was mentioned half-way through the evening, Jon started to complain that it wasn't fair to have our wedding on the 29th February because it was on a Monday and he wouldn't be able to have a lot to drink.

Beth also piped up that Ashley and Samantha were at school that day and might not be able to get the time off. Paul and I explained that we had picked this date as it was a leap year day. It was a unique and special day and we would have to wait another four years until the next one.

They still kept moaning, asking us to change the date. I was beginning to get annoyed. It was supposed to be mine and Paul's special day and they were upset because they couldn't have a big party and get drunk, or because it didn't fit in with their kids.

The silly thing about Jon's objection to our wedding date was that he had his own business, so I'm sure my brother could have arranged to take a couple of days off. Looking back, I think they were trying to ruin everything for me so that I didn't get married and were maybe hoping that Paul would get fed up and leave me.

The wedding arrangements we had planned were simple: we would get married at Chesterfield Register Office at 10.30am, just the two of us and two witnesses, and then we would have a reception with everyone invited. Then we would just go away somewhere for one day.

But even that was out of the question because no one would look after the dogs for us, even for just one day. And it was mentioned that it didn't seem right that we were only having two witnesses in the room with us. They said: 'what's the point of waiting outside?'

We explained that we did not have much money and so we were having a "cheap and cheerful" theme for the wedding, trying to lighten the mood. But they were determined to disagree with whatever we had planned.

We explained that the money we were saving by not paying extra for a bigger room at Chesterfield Register Office would help to pay for the evening reception, disco and buffet.

In the end, I was so mad and upset, I just tried to change the subject and we eventually went home.

The following day, after going over everything that had been said by my family, Paul and I decided that it was our wedding and we would do what we wanted. So we decided that after we had been to the registrar, we would go on holiday for a few days with the dogs and not have a reception. The money saved from the reception paid for the holiday.

After a few weeks, nothing else had been mentioned about the wedding; not even Dad mentioned it. Until one day, when Beth asked me for a proper invitation card so that the kids could take it to school to be allowed the day off.

So I went along with it and not only wrote invitation cards for Jon, Beth and kids, but also to my sister and her family.

Soon afterwards, I kept getting text messages from Beth and Sally, saying who was going and who wasn't, who might be going and who didn't know if they could get time off work. In the end, I was so fed up with the constant bickering and text messages. So I sent a message to all of them, asking to reply to the RSVP on the bottom of their invites by the end of the week so I knew who was going and who was not. It was the beginning of December and only three months until the wedding.

That was when it all kicked off again.

I had been suffering with an ear infection all week, so I wasn't very well, and I was getting constant phone calls and text messages about the wedding, which I'd stopped answering because I was ill. In the end, Paul answered my phone. It was Beth. Paul told her to stop hassling me and said I was ill with an ear infection, but she just ranted and raved and in the end, Jon came on the phone too, threatening Paul.

I was upset and angry. I decided that we would cancel all the plans we'd made and just get married and then take off, just us and the dogs.

Over the weekend, I wrote letters to my sister and brother to explain that we were cancelling the plans for the wedding and how upset I was about it.

I am writing to inform you that we have now cancelled our wedding plans for Monday 29th February 2016.

We apologise for any inconvenience to you with your work and other commitments but we think that it is for the best. It seems that there is too much friction and upset within the family. All that I wanted was for my family to be there for me on my happy and special day. But it seems that I'm asking too much for all of you to be happy for me and to stop the petty arguments and bickering for just one day.

It has been a very painful thing for me to write to you and tell you that the wedding is cancelled but I have given it a lot of thought over the past few days and I realise that it has gone too far and someone can only take so much.

Some people have commented that they are disgusted that I'm wearing my Mum's wedding dress. The only person that it matters to is my Dad, and I asked him if it was okay from the beginning. And he said he would be proud of me to wear it. Maybe you could stop and think about how I feel. You both had my Mum on your wedding days and she will not be there for me on mine.

And as for not being there for any of you, I have always been there for every one of you: my Mum, Nanna, Dad, Grandad, uncles, brother, sister, sister-in-law, brother-in-law, nephews, niece and cousins. If it's babysitting, taxi service, helping out or just listening, I've been there.

I know I've made mistakes in the past, but haven't we all? But I never judge you or throw it in your face every time there's an argument – that's all I get. There's no one sorrier than me that things have happened and I wish I could change it. But now I'm settled, happy and safe. I can't understand why my family cannot be happy for me.

I will still be visiting my Dad, but please can you give some consideration for him and not keep arguing when we visit. That applies to Adam too.

I just wish to get on with my life and don't want all the upset all the time. I thought this wedding would have bought the family together for the day, but it just seems to push everyone further away.

Once again, we apologise for the inconvenience.

Lisa

After Jon received the letter, he phoned me and asked why I hadn't talked to him before writing the letter saying that the wedding wasn't going ahead.

We kept getting reports from Dad over the following days when we visited him, about what Jon, Beth and Sally were saying about me and Paul.

Every time Paul and I went round to visit Dad, we would only be in the house for a couple of minutes before his phone would ring. It would be Beth, telling my Dad to go round and look after her kids, or that she wanted him to go to a shop, or some other excuse so he had to go. She was playing a childish and selfish game.

They found out, probably through Dad, that we were still getting married and so they started talking to us again. We decided that we would book the Highfield Pub and have a buffet after we got married, and then, when Paul and I left to go on the holiday we had booked, the family could stay in the pub and have as much to drink as they wanted, because it wasn't far for them to walk home.

Dad said he would pay for it, seeing as Paul and I had paid for everything else. It was his wedding present to us.

Paul and I went to the Highfield pub the following day and booked the room and a buffet for the wedding date.

A few days later, we heard that Jon was accusing us of spending the money that Dad had given us for the buffet on ourselves.

We took the receipt from the pub and showed Dad, and told him to give a copy of it to Jon.

I'd just had enough of them and told them. We cancelled the buffet and room at the pub and we lost half the money because we had paid it in full.

The instigators behind all the trouble-causing were Beth and Sally.

They have not spoken to me and Paul since then.

They knew we had no money and were organising the wedding as cheaply as we could.

My colleague Rosie and her boyfriend ended up being our two witnesses.

Rosie took the photographs because she enjoys doing photography in her spare time.

Rosie's boyfriend had a blue BMW and he drove me to the registry office.

I made my own bouquet of flowers and Rosie had a small bouquet and a corsage.

My dress ended up being from eBay and cost £20. Originally, I was going to wear my Mum's wedding dress which she had given me many years ago and I had saved. I'd had it altered, but only a few weeks before the wedding, I found that nobody would dry clean the dress because it was vintage, so at the last minute, I had to look for a replacement.

I was gutted, because it was a way my Mum could be there with me. I'd asked my Dad if he minded me wearing it. I didn't want to upset him because it was Mum's dress, but he said it was a lovely idea.

Not long after I'd asked Dad, I was informed that my sister-in-law had said she wanted the dress. Even though she hadn't previously known that it existed, she now wanted it for her daughter. There was no way I was giving it to her.

Paul's suit and shirt were from the Next catalogue.

Adam and Sean's shirts and ties and Paul's tie were from Primark.

The wedding cake was made by a lady who had a stall on Chesterfield market. We just had a round sponge cake and a dozen or so fancy cupcakes, decorated in the colours of royal and light blue to match our colour theme. She made two icing figures to look like me and Paul in our wedding outfits, and the four dogs were also made in icing. It was wonderful.

Sadly though, a few weeks before the wedding, we lost Ellie, our Westie dog. I was very upset, because it was another connection with Mum, as she had chosen Ellie.

Our wedding rings were from Argos.

We went to the Olde House Pub for a meal, along with the two witnesses, Adam and his boyfriend, Sean.

When I added up the entire cost: for the rings, clothes, flowers, licence, cake, the meal after the wedding, dress and our holiday, it cost just under two thousand pounds.

We had a lovely day. I was hoping that my brother would have a change of heart and turn up, but he didn't. Paul's two nieces and their boyfriends did though, which was nice.

After our meal at the Olde House, we went back to the flat and got changed, collected the dogs and went on holiday to Cropton, North Yorkshire. We stayed in a log cabin in a forest. We had a wonderful week.

Me and Paul: our wedding

Adam at our wedding.

I made the bouquet myself.

With Adam and My Dad at the wedding.

Getting ready for the wedding.

At the wedding with Adam and Sean.

Chapter 14: Gypsy Woman

When me and Paul moved into the flat at Wyedale court, Adam came with us, and also his boyfriend, Sean.

Everything was okay at first but after a few months, Adam started playing up. He would go to work and leave the door unlocked. When we did the weekly shopping and came home from work the following day, we'd find that Adam and Sean had eaten everything so we had to go shopping again.

I did have words with Adam and, I told him I wasn't choosing between him and Paul; I wasn't getting involved with it.

In the end, in April 2016, Adam moved out and went to live in a flat on Chester Street with Sean.

We were fine in the flat. There were a few incidents – the neighbours above us had a young daughter who would roller skate around in their flat, and I don't think they had carpets on the floor, so you can imagine the noise.

Also, the man downstairs had a few mental health issues and would press the door buzzer in the middle of the night because he'd forgotten his key.

There was always something going off, because it was right next to a busy shopping centre and carpark.

Every time we took the dogs a walk, we would feel like the Pied Piper, with groups of kids following us so they could stroke and play with the dogs. It would take thirty minutes or more just to go on a normal ten-minute walk.

Everything was going fine until Gary started to hang about in the area and I didn't dare to go out on my own, even to walk the dogs.

In November 2016, we moved and ended up in a flat at Kingswood Close, Dunston.

This time, the flat was a duplex, a house split in two with one flat upstairs and one flat downstairs; it also had a shared garden. We were in the upstairs flat.

We settled in and things were going fine. We decided to put up a fence halfway down the garden so we could let the dogs out without disturbing the neighbour. We got permission from the council and the neighbour also agreed and signed the papers to say she agreed.

I got in touch with my cousin, Robert to ask him if he would do the work of putting up the fence. He came to measure up for the fencing and other stuff we needed and quoted us a total of £700, including the labour.

We didn't have much money and we told him we would be in touch to let him know when we had the money.

This was in January 2017. We discussed it with Dad, who said he would lend us the money. We got back in touch with Robert so he could do the work straight away. As it was winter, he didn't have much work on, so we thought it would also help him out. We gave him the full £700 and he said that he would start at the beginning of February. He didn't turn up on the day. We tried to get in touch with him but he wouldn't answer his phone or reply to any messages.

In the end, after a couple of days, we managed to catch him. He said that he was sorry but when we gave him the money he had gone into town to put the money into the bank but when he got to town, the money had disappeared. He'd lost it.

'Why didn't you just tell us what had happened instead of ignoring us?' I asked him.

To help him out, we told him that he could either pay our money back in a weekly amount, or pay it back by putting a fence panel up in our garden whenever he got the money to buy one.

Robert agreed to come and do the work and arranged to start in the following couple of weeks.

Again, he never showed up. By this time, we had found out that he had probably gambled the money away.

He avoided us altogether; we called round to his house and tried everything to talk to him. Paul was mad, and so was I because I had to explain to my Dad about what had happened, which was awkward and I felt like I had stolen the money. My Dad was very understanding though, and just told us to pay it back when we could.

In the end, we got a county court order on Robert. I didn't like to but we had given him several chances.

We still haven't heard from him and have not received a penny back.

We gave up because it was costing us money to take him to court, as we both were working and he was just ignoring the summons and papers served on him.

As for the fencing, Paul and I bought some plastic barrier fencing and poles and put that up so the dogs could go onto the garden.

But this caused problems with the neighbour, who had started to be funny and awkward. She was a bit odd anyway – she used to walk about in the garden wearing virtually nothing and so Paul was uncomfortable about being in the garden because he didn't want any aggravation from her.

She was adamant that her bins went on our side of the garden and she accused us of taking up some of her side, even though the council had visited our property and showed us where the fence was to go.

Every time we came home or took the dogs into the garden, she would be there. She complained about the dogs barking, so we had a monitor fitted in the flat that linked to our phones and while I was at work in between my jobs, I kept checking it. On several occasions, I did see the dogs start barking, but that was after she had banged the bedroom window with a long pole. She was scaring the dogs and making us stressed each day.

So in July 2017, we moved to Model Village, Creswell, near Worksop.

Chapter 15: Mr Smith

2017 was also another mad, packed year.

I was diagnosed with very high blood pressure Is there any wonder? I was given medication for it.

I was also having trouble with my stomach and was referred to Mr Smith, a consultant at the Chesterfield Royal Hospital. I was told that I had an ovarian cyst.

My appointments with Mr Smith didn't go very well.

At the first appointment, when I arrived with Paul, we were told that Mr Smith was running an hour late and the waiting room was busy. So we told the receptionist on the desk that we would go down to the cafe to have a drink and would come back in an hour. We returned and informed the receptionist, who told us to go into the waiting room, where this time, there was only one person waiting.

We were waiting for over thirty minutes or more and no one was called in. I was getting more and more stressed and anxious and needed to "go".

It didn't help me either that the radio was on in the waiting room. It was a chat show discussing women being sexually abused in the workplace. I didn't think it was very appropriate in a women's health clinic. And because of my past, it wasn't helping.

A nurse went to tell Mr Smith that we were waiting, and he happened to be in the room where we were standing. He was on the phone and when the nurse explained that we'd been waiting a long time, he finished his call and slammed the phone down.

I was told yet again to go back into the waiting room and was called to see Mr Smith about 5-10 minutes later.

By this time, I was really anxious and panicking and I told Paul to talk to Mr Smith as I was too worked up to speak. Mr Smith was arrogant and I felt as though I was an inconvenience. He couldn't be bothered to read through my medical notes to see why I had been referred to him; he said that he didn't know why I was there and asked me to explain.

I'd been referred by my doctor for what I thought was a scan, as my doctor had already done an internal pelvis examination and had taken swabs that came back clear. I was also having trouble with my periods and was in chronic pain.

So I was very surprised when Mr Smith asked me to remove my clothes and lie on the bed. He then proceeded to carry out an internal examination and take swabs, without explaining what he was doing and why. I'm also sure that he didn't wear any gloves.

I asked Paul to sit with me and hold my hand as I was scared when I realised what he was doing. He was not gentle and I was in great pain while he was doing this and I was in pain for the rest of the day. I also started bleeding afterwards, for about a week.

I got dressed and he then Mr Smith said that he would book me in for a scan. I can't remember much else as I was upset and in pain. I just wanted to go home.

He was also arrogant and rude to Paul. Half way through the appointment, he asked who Paul was. You'd think he would have asked at the start.

The next appointment I had with Mr Smith was about five months later. He did seem to have a better attitude towards me.

He explained that the ovarian cyst that had showed up on the first scan I'd had had now shrunk, which meant it was nothing serious. He said that I didn't need surgery, and just to keep an eye on it, he would arrange for another scan in six months. He then turned to me and asked if he could do an internal examination.

I looked at Paul, who was sitting next to me. I was surprised. I turned back to Mr Smith and said no.

Mr Smith just turned away and confirmed the date of the future scan and told me that if I had any problems, to go and see my GP. He didn't ask why I'd said no to an internal scan or explain why he'd wanted to do the examination.

As I left the consultation with Paul and we were walking through the hospital, we discussed what had happened and decided to report him to the Assistance & Complaints Services at Chesterfield Royal Hospital. I felt that something was not right and I was very upset.

The ladies who worked in the Complaints Service were very helpful and empathetic. They took the details of my complaint and arranged for me to have a meeting with the clinical director of the Women & Children's Division and the matron of the Women's Health unit.

At the meeting, they just made excuses up and defended Mr Smith. They say he definitely wore gloves as all doctors wear gloves.

'How do you know? You weren't there,' we said.

They told us that Mr Smith was a highly professional consultant in his job, and that he did everything correctly and to the letter.

And as for thinking I was going for a scan on the first appointment, the clinical director said that when you lie on a couch, you should know that the doctor will be doing an examination.

'But you also lie down on a couch if you're having a scan,' I replied.

(By that example, if you lie down on a bed, is it okay if a man rapes you?)

I asked if could be examined by a woman. She replied that it wasn't always practical, as there wasn't always an available woman doctor.

They made me feel like I was only complaining because he was a man and that he had upset me because of my past history of rape and abuse. I told them that I had been examined by male doctors before and was not discriminating, but that there was something about my examination by Mr Smith that was just not right.

I told them that the rest of the hospital staff had been really wonderful.

The matron said that changes had been made regarding the radio in the waiting room. She had taken on board my suggestions of what radio stations to play and would be more careful in future.

They asked if they could use my complaint in learning materials and magazines to help educate other doctors and nurses about patients' experience.

So at least something good came out of it.

Chapter 16: Goodbye Dad

In 2017, Adam and Sean moved into a house on St. Thomas Street in Brampton, not long before we moved to Model Village in Creswell.

In the early hours of one summer morning, I received a phone call from Adam, saying he was sorry but he was on a bridge in the town centre and he was going to jump off.

I rushed to reach him. Creswell is about twenty to thirty minutes by car from Chesterfield.

When I got into town, I saw the police cars and police officers. They had blocked off each end of the Chesterfield by-pass and were talking to Adam to try to get him to come off the bridge. I was devastated and I think I aged about twenty years that night.

The police wouldn't let me go to Adam until he was safely off the bridge. They told me that if there was no one to watch him in the next twenty-four hours, then he would be taken to hospital. I said that I would take him home with me, so I had to phone work to say I wasn't going in.

This wasn't the first time Adam had phoned me in the early hours to say he had done something. At the beginning of the year, he had tried to slit his wrists and I went to his house to talk to him.

A couple of weeks after the bridge incident, I received another phone call in the early hours of the morning. It was Jon and Beth, saying that Adam was at their house and they needed me to come and get him.

I couldn't believe it. I got into the car with Paul and went to fetch Adam. We apologised to Jon and Beth.

Adam was drunk. He said he thought that if he could get us all together, then we would start talking and be friends again. It didn't happen. All that it did was cause more friction and it was very uncomfortable and awkward situation.

All Jon and Beth did was to make sarcastic comments. We got Adam outside and he kicked off, saying he was going to do something to himself, so we took him to A&E.

After waiting ages, the crisis team came to assess Adam. Paul and I had to leave, because we were both due at work in a couple of hours. And I didn't dare to have any more time off work. We couldn't afford to lose the money, and my work colleague, Rosie had started to be funny with me.

Adam was sent home not long afterwards and was given an appointment for further help.

We were shattered.

In August, the following month, we had yet another phone call from Adam. Apparently he'd had an argument with Sean, and Sean's dad had supposedly thrown Adam out, so he said he was walking the streets and was upset.

I was worried that Adam would do something silly, so we made the trip to Chesterfield again to search for him. We couldn't find him, so we phoned the police, who came out to St. Thomas Street. While we told a police officer what had happened and how worried we were for Adam's safety, another police officer visited Sean's parents' house.

When this officer returned, he said that Adam was there and was alright – he was laughing and joking with Sean and his parents.

I was aghast: absolutely surprised, shocked and embarrassed. We apologised to the police for wasting their time.

I ran off crying, I was so upset and exhausted. Paul ran after me and eventually caught up with me. We sat together and Paul calmed me down. I felt like I couldn't cope any more. I felt so hurt and sad about Adam.

Paul was angry with Adam for putting me through so much stress over the past year. He told Adam later that if we got any more phone calls in the middle of the night, we would just call the police and let them sort him out.

We couldn't keep getting up in the middle of the night and then going to work in the early hours of the morning, traveling to Chesterfield. I was cleaning several properties all day and driving too.

That did the trick, because he never did it again.

Around October 2017, we applied to become foster carers.

We filled in all the forms, got our references, had our medical assessments and interviews and everything seemed to be going fine. Then, out of the blue, the people from the fostering organisation came out to see us and told us that they were very sorry but we couldn't foster for them – and they refused to tell us why.

Paul phoned up the Derbyshire fostering services and asked them for more information. They told him that it could be because I'd been put on safeguarding at the time of the Michael incident. Or maybe it was because it was a private company. You usually find that they encourage lots of people to apply to get funding from the government, and then only a handful of people are given the places. In other words, it was like a con.

I was upset and devastated: this is what I had always wanted to do. The Derbyshire foster services said we could try to apply with them, but I would probably have to go through some psychological assessments and other tests.

We said we would wait and think about it. Paul didn't want to put me through the stress of going through my whole past again.

This stressful year didn't end there.

On October 24th, our pug Tio died. She was nine years old. We were really upset; we had lost a member of the family.

Tio was a proper diva, everyone loved her. When we took her out, especially on holiday, strangers would come up and ask to take her photo. Tio would just sit there with her best pose and she acted like the queen of pugs.

She had only been with me for three years but it seemed like I'd had her for a lot longer. When I got her, she was in a poor state. Her former owners only sold her to me because she was no good for breeding anymore and was getting too old.

She was also kept in milk to feed litters of puppies from other dogs. She had been recently spayed when I went to fetch her and she still had stitches in, which the vet said was illegal to do. Her belly was nearly touching the floor. Also she didn't like to have a lead on her – she would be happy just plodding along behind me.

We still miss her today. In the three years we had her, she made a very big impression on us.

A few days later, on October 27th, we got a phone call from my sister-in-law, Beth, saying that my Dad had been taken in hospital.

I had spoken to Dad on the phone a couple of days before. He said he'd been away to Skegness over the weekend with Jon, Beth and the kids and that he'd come home feeling ill. He said he'd got sickness and diarrhoea.

We visited Dad in the hospital and he looked very ill. Jon and Beth were there too, and so were Sally, Tim and their son James.

The atmosphere was very uncomfortable.

Sally wanted to take charge as usual, and Beth was trying to compete with her.

Jon and I went in to see Dad, as only a couple of people were allowed to see him at a time. Dad hardly spoke. He just asked if I was okay and if Paul was with me. Afterwards, Jon took me to one side and we tried to patch things up between us. It worked in a way. I thought that maybe I was getting my brother back, but as soon as he got back with Beth and Sally, he hardly spoke.

Adam was camping in the Lake District at the time, and when I phoned to tell him about his Grandad, he came straight back to Chesterfield.

The doctors said that they had given Dad something to make him more comfortable and were taking him to the intensive care ward. There was nothing else we could do, so we went home.

We went back to the hospital on the Saturday morning. The doctors said they had done some tests on Dad and that he had a form of cancer, which was too far advanced to operate on. He couldn't have treatment because of his condition and he had only one kidney, so they couldn't do anything apart from to make him comfortable.

Adam and I went in to see Dad. He wasn't conscious and he was wired up to some machines. He was in a bad way. I said my goodbyes to him there and then.

Later on in the evening, we got a call from Beth to say that they were going to turn the off the machines that were keeping Dad alive.

I had already said my goodbyes that morning and I knew that Dad was not conscious either. Also, Beth and

Sally were at his bedside, so I knew I wouldn't get to be near him anyway. I couldn't be doing with the false tears. Adam called round again to see Dad about 11pm.

All that night, I expected a phone call. The following morning, I phoned the hospital to ask about Dad. The nurses were a bit surprised and asked if my family had been in touch. They said my Dad had passed away at 11.15pm last night.

In the next few days, I tried to find out where they had taken Dad. Eventually, I got a call from Lorraine, the lady who worked with Mum at the Co-op, to say that my Dad was at the Co-op funeral parlour in Staveley.

Lorraine also kept me informed about my Dad's funeral arrangements as my brother and sister didn't tell me anything.

I was mad and upset – he was my Dad too.

They decided to scatter my Mum's, my Dad's, my Nana's and my Grandad's ashes at Brimington Crematorium.

The ashes had previously been in my Dad's garden, in pots with roses planted beside them.

Also, my Dad had made a will – and it was probably a good thing he did.

I knew what was in the original will because I had to write it for him, but when I moved out with Paul and they fell out with me, Beth took Dad to change his will at the solicitors.

Apparently, Jon was made executor of his will.

My Dad's house was sold and emptied. Before it was completely emptied, I was asked if I wanted to see if there was anything I wanted before they skipped it all. Paul came with me. I could see that the family had picked through everything, but I didn't care – all I wanted was a picture that he'd painted. He'd painted loads of pictures and they used to be kept in the spare bedroom, but when I looked, there were not many left. And I was told I could only pick two for me and two for Adam.

As I walked around the house that had been my home since I was sixteen, my brother and sister followed me around from room to room. I felt like I was some stranger and they were watching in case I pinched something.

I'd lived there a lot longer than either of them.

I didn't really stay long and as I left, I thanked Jon for dealing with the funeral and the house and I appreciated what he had done. I told him that if there was anything that he wanted, then he could call any time.

I was extending him an olive branch.

But sadly, I've not heard anything from him. I know that one day he will need someone, if only to talk to, and I hope that he's not too proud to call me.

I just want him to know that there is somebody out there for him who does care.

My Dad

Paul and Adam

Chapter 17: The Priory & The Flat from Hell

By April 2018, I was starting to feel depressed again. It had been a tough year. With the loss of my Dad, scattering my Mum's and grandparents' ashes and being refused as a foster carer, I was already feeling low. And by this time, Paul was working for an agency, so he was in and out of work. At work, I was fed up with the way I was being treated. Rosie was being funny with me and I found out that she had been constantly lying to me.

In the end, after nearly ten years of working for the company, I handed in my notice. I was due to receive my share of inheritance from the sale of my Dad's house, so we could pay off bills we owed and I wouldn't need to work for a while. I could have a break and get my head sorted.

We went on a few holidays with the dogs. By this time, we had another dog, a Labrador puppy called Marley. We went to Presteigne, Wales, Chipping, near Preston and Keldy in North Yorkshire. We also went on holiday to Scotland and visited Gretna Green and Loch Ness.

Marley went to boot camp while we went on holiday to Scotland, as she was growing and pulling more strongly on her lead. We dropped her off and didn't hear anything from the dog trainer for a couple of days.

When we got in touch with them, they said that Marley was doing well and that she was sitting in the office with the staff or was in the kitchen. It sounded like they weren't really doing any training with her. It cost £350 for the week and when we picked her up, it took us two weeks to calm her down and now she is very nervous.

We also made a trip to the outskirts of London. We stayed in a cabin near Royal Wotton Bassett. Our stay was to tie in with an appointment I had to attend at the private Priory Hospital in Southgate, to see a Dr Brennen. This was due to the case with Michael and the NHS Trust. My solicitor arranged the appointment for me to have an independent psychological assessment, to determine the amount of compensation.

The Priory is a very big building and it felt very intimidating I was told to sit in a waiting area until I was called, because all the doors were security code locked.

Dr Brennan called me in to his office and asked me lots of questions, going through my past history, my family and my feelings. He then let Paul join me and asked him a few questions too.

Paul told me later that while he was sitting waiting for me, a male member of staff asked him to follow him and started taking him down one of the corridors. Paul followed, and as he was walking, he asked if I was okay.

The man asked Paul who he was talking about and realised that he had got the wrong person. He took Paul back to the waiting area. It looked like Paul had a close call – he was nearly admitted into the Priory!

Also, while he was waiting, he saw a famous celebrity who was in the newspapers around that time.

While we were in the area, we went to see my solicitor in Harlow. I went to see her to thank her for all her help and took her some flowers.

On one of the mornings when we were staying in the cabin, we couldn't get out because the door handle was broken. I had to climb through the bedroom window and open the cabin door from the outside!

For Christmas 2018, we went on holiday again and were to spend the Christmas week on the Norfolk coast in a boat that was converted into a holiday place. It looked lovely on the photos on the holiday site and we thought it would be something special and different for Christmas.

When we arrived, it had been raining all day, and there were massive pot holes going down the lane to the boat which were like small ponds.

As we walked into the cabin, we realised it was dark, dingy, cold and full of cobwebs. There were only a couple of small electric heaters and the place was cramped and cluttered with the owner's personal belongings.

The windows were black and mouldy and the curtains were blowing as though the window was open.

The kitchen and bathroom were in need of a deep clean. And it was supposed to have been decorated for Christmas for us too. There were a few baubles that looked like they had been thrown on the sides and a two foot tree with shreds of tinsel and odd baubles. It was definitely not worth the £1000 we had to pay.

When we went out the following day, we found that the door was warped and rotten from the weather and a piece of wood had fallen off the door.

The beach and surrounding area was lovely. We visited Sandringham Estate and we saw the Queen, who waved as she went past in her car from the church.

On Christmas Eve, after a couple of days, we couldn't stand it any longer, so we packed up and went home to spend Christmas day at home.

Previously in November, we had moved yet again, from Creswell to a flat at Queen Street, Brimington. It was privately rented and we'd let it through an estate agent. It was the flat from hell.

The day after we moved in, we discovered a gas leak. The gas company came out and mended it but we were worried, because everything was supposed to have been checked before we moved in. As the days went by, we discovered more and more problems. It was a nightmare. After a couple of weeks, we went to the estate agent with a list of complaints. We also went to the Citizens Advice Centre for advice about what to do.

Here are some of our complaints:
Tiles loose in the fireplace.

Loose boards on the floor near sink.
The shower didn't work.
The bath had small holes in it.

A couple of doors didn't shut. One was the bathroom – it had no door handle

There was a plug socket which you couldn't use, as a radiator was half covering it.

The bath was leaking underneath, and only resting on bricks.

The toilets were disgusting and it took us ages to get them clean.

The sink in the bathroom was coming loose from the wall.

The fan was not working in the kitchen.

There was a strange noise in the kitchen which sounded like a washing machine upstairs, but when we asked the woman who lived in the flat above, she wasn't in at the times of the noise.

The wrong gas certificate was issued for our boiler.

The electrics were not safe and we hired two electricians confirm to it. One walked out in disgust and refused to touch anything.

It was advertised for £450 PCM, but the estate agent was charging us £475. It was even advertised in her window as £450. The excuse given was that it was a misprint.

And other minor faults...

I felt uncomfortable in the place; it was creepy and cold all the time. It was making me really depressed. I just wanted to move. We had paid a full six months' rent up front, but we didn't care. It was so bad, we were willing to lose the money.

We put our names on the council list and in March 2019, we moved to Hanbury Court, Holme Hall.

Before we left the Citizens Advice Centre, we were advised to report our rented property to the environmental health department, which we did.

Chapter 18: Hanbury

Moving to Holme Hall , I thought we were going to get a quiet life and a bit of peace. But it seemed not.

Holme Hall, let's say, has got a bit of a reputation, but not as bad as Grangewood.

The block of flats where we live is fairly quiet though, and the people are nice.

Since moving here in March, the police have been around our street most weeks, from drug raids to knife crime incidents, to domestic issues and car fires.

We keep ourselves to ourselves and we have no trouble. Everyone speaks to us when we take the dogs for a walk and I feel okay here.

There were a lot of forensic crime officers on the street one week, because of the hunt for a local man who been missing for a number of days. They found some dismembered parts of him around the town – it was big news for a few weeks.

One day, our utilities provider told us to check our gas and electric meters. They are smart meters, so usually we don't need to check them, but the readings weren't tallying up and we had to have a new one installed.

So Paul went to check the meters, which are situated outside our flat, down a passageway in a small hallway shared with next door. Nobody was living next door. It had recently been renovated and was up for sale.

'Just look at this,' Paul said. He was holding a plastic bag with some white powder in it.

'Where did you get that from?'

'It was stuck in the electric box.'

'What is it?'

'I've no idea' Paul said. 'But it's white powder in a plastic bag – it's got to be something dodgy!'

'Just flush it down the toilet,' I said.

'No – what if they come back for it – whoever left it there.'

We talked about phoning the police, but I didn't want the police coming to the flat, because it might cause trouble for us if anyone in the area found out. So we decided to take it to the police station in town. We put the bag in an envelope, and I put it in my pocket.

In the car, on the way to the police station, I said: 'I hope we don't get pulled over by the police now. They are not going to believe that we're taking it to the police station to hand it in.'

When we arrived at the station, we explained to the woman on the front desk how we found the suspicious package and why we bought it to them. She looked at us as though it was some kind of prank, then she took our details and put some gloves on and took it off us.

'I'll go and see the sergeant,' she said. She wasn't gone long.

'Don't worry about it, it's nothing,' she said on her return. 'The sergeant's disposed of it.'

'What if we get any more of them?' Paul asked.

'Just return them', she said, as though we were ordering the packages.

'Where to?' replied Paul.

'Don't worry about it, it's nothing,' she said.

Outside, we both looked at one another and said: 'That was a waste of time.'

One day we decided to go to the Arndale shopping centre in Manchester, as I'd never been before.

We had almost finished looking around the shopping centre, but Paul wanted to look in the HMV shop before we went home.

As we were walking around the corner to the shop, we were met by a swarm of people, all running towards us. They were shouting and yelling at us to get out. We didn't know what was happening. Paul grabbed my hand and started to run with me towards the nearest exit. If we had not turned and ran, we would have been trampled to death.

When we got outside on the street, we saw the bomb squad. The armed police had just arrived and were getting ready to go in.

The street was crowded with people who were confused and panic-stricken.

Paul and I walked around the building, to see if we could find out what was happening. Through the glass doors, you could see it was empty except for the police officers and security. We asked some people if they knew what was happening and we were told that apparently, a young man had stood up on one of the tables in the restaurant area, took his top off and started shouting for everybody to be quiet and listen to him because he had something important to tell them.

People said that he had a gun and as soon as it happened, people started running.

After a while, people started to drift back inside the shopping centre. The police and staff were saying it was a false alarm and that everything was okay.

We thought it was strange – why would hundreds of people panic and run?

We collected our car from the car park and went home.

On the way home, getting out of Manchester was a nightmare. We kept listening to the news station on the radio, but nothing was mentioned.

By the time we got home, I was shaking and I felt sick with the thought of what could have happened. I thought about those poor souls who were at the Manchester arena concert on the night of the bombing – what it would have been like for them? It must have been dreadful.

A few days later, we heard that a relative of a friend had been there at the time and was sitting straight opposite the young man. They saw everything.

The young man did stand on the table and take his top off and tell everyone to listen to him, and he did produce a gun, waving it about. When the security guards ran towards him, he jumped off the table, collected his bag and ran off into the panicked crowds.

It was reported in the news that it was a false alarm and no gun was found. But they wouldn't find a gun if the man had run off with it and they hadn't caught him, would they?

A few weeks after that, we went shopping in Meadowhall shopping centre, Sheffield. I've been here many times before, but this time, I started to have a panic attack because of the incident in the Arndale Centre. I just wanted to go home. Once I was home, I felt stupid and pathetic.

What were the chances of it happening again?

Chapter 19: For the Love of Dogs

My story wouldn't be complete without mentioning my love of dogs.

I've had various pets over the years, from guinea pigs, rabbits, budgies, parrot, gerbils and even chickens and a duck called Roger.

But dogs are really the ones that have made a big impression on me. From being a baby, they have always been in my life, starting with Simba, the Shetland Sheepdog.

My Mum got Simba before my sister and I were born. One night, she won at bingo, and with the winnings, she bought Simba. She looked exactly like Lassie, the dog from the films. When I was very young, I can remember that the dog had a lump on its head and Mum told us always to be careful of it. Sadly, Simba died because of the tumour.

We then had another dog, called Scamp. He was also a Shetland Sheepdog, but a miniature version. Scamp was really playful and we would occasionally dress him up. He was only young when he died. The vet said they thought it was from some kind of poison. The only thing we could think of was that we lived at Dowdeswell Street at the time, next to the field and after the dog had been on the field, he would constantly lick his feet. We think maybe he caught something off the field.

We couldn't have any more pets after Scamp, because when my brother was born, he suffered very badly with eczema and asthma.

My uncle Mike bought a little dog, an Italian greyhound. They look like small whippets – they are really skinny, with hardly any hair, and he thought that it would be an ideal pet for us because the very short coat wouldn't upset my brother's asthma.

Unfortunately, it didn't work out because the dog had lots of health problems of his own. But he could run! We called him Tim.

My Dad used to take him for a walk and the dog would slip his lead and run off to the park, but he would always make his way back home. We'd hear scratching at the door. Half an hour afterwards, my Dad would walk in the house.

'The dogs gone,' he'd say. But the dog was already lying in front of the fire!

Tim's ears were paper-thin and very fragile. When it was cold, his ears would rip and then he'd shake his head, making his ears would bleed.

Then he started to have fits. I remember coming home from work one day and having to hold him because he was having a fit, and he would bang into the walls and furniture.

We took him to the vets and they said that his condition would get worse, and his fits were getting more frequent. So we had to put him down, because it would have been cruel to let him go on suffering like that.

When I left home and moved into the flat with Gary, he got me a Jack Russell dog called Max. He was supposed to be a birthday present but we got him free as the previous owners wanted to get rid of him.

Max was a lovely dog and like myself, suffered at the hands of Gary. But thankfully, we both escaped. When Adam was born and growing up, Max was very protective over him. He would walk at the side of Adam's pushchair and stand guard if another dog came close to him. In the house, when Adam was asleep, Max would lie nearby and stay there until Adam woke up, When Adam cried, Max would howl until I went to pick Adam up. I don't know what the neighbours thought with the noise.

Max was quite old when he died.

Not long after we lost Max, my Mum went halves on paying for another dog with me. She liked West Highland terriers. We got one from my Mum's cousin who breeds them. He only had two left, one bitch and one dog; we wanted the dog. We called him Charlie.

The following day, we took the puppy to the vet for a check-up and injections. The vet, Mr Taylor, said that everything was okay. We took Charlie back to the vet a few days afterwards to be microchipped, and this time, we saw a veterinary nurse.

After Charlie was registered with the microchip, we asked her why he was crawling along the floor a lot. She looked underneath the dog and laughed out loud.

'You've got a bitch, not a dog.' We couldn't believe it – the breeder and a vet had told us we had a dog.

'Didn't you look?' the nurse asked.

'You don't keep looking at a dog's privates all the time, and with being a puppy, I thought they would grow bigger,' my Mum replied.

'And it cocks its leg up when it wees,' I added.

As we were leaving the vets, I said: 'We came in with a dog and we're coming out with a bitch. Next time we come again, we'll probably come out with a rabbit.'

We renamed the dog Ellie.

Ellie had a good long life with us and was about twelve years old when she died of kidney failure.

Adam kept pestering us for his own dog, so Jon and I took him to fetch a dog we'd seen advertised in a local paper. It was a Scottish terrier and we went to fetch her on a cold, rainy evening. It was dark when we got to the house and the owners went to fetch the dog from the shed outside. Adam said that he would keep the dog and promised to look after it.

When we got home, we noticed that the dog was snuffling but we thought it was because she was wet and cold. But on closer inspection, we saw that she only had half a nose – one of her nostrils hadn't formed right.

We gave her a good bath and called her Meg. She was such a lovely dog, with a good temperament and a little shy. And of course, I ended up looking after her.

Adam kept saying: 'Can we swap her? She's faulty.'

'No, you can't swap dogs like that, she's part of the family now. And if it was so easy to swap things, wouldn't you think they'd start with kids?' I would say.

It was only in jest.

Sadly, she died when she was about eight years old, while I was on holiday in Czech Republic.

While I had Ellie and Meg, I decided to get another dog, a pug, Oscar. He is a right character. He thinks he's a Rottweiler in a pug's body.

He also likes to sing and watch the TV. His favourite programmes are Paul O'Grady's *For the Love of Dogs*, the 'meerkats' adverts and police programmes. All the way through, he barks at the dogs and the police chases. As soon as the theme music comes on, he sits in front of the telly. We still have Oscar – he's nine now.

After Meg died, I saw an advert for a black pug called Tio. I've already mentioned her in a previous chapter. We bought her from a puppy farm – she'd been used for breeding.

We had her for three years; they were definitely the best three years of her life, because we spoiled her rotten. She took everything in her stride and she used to look after the other dogs, as though it was still her job to be a mother.

When Adam was living at home and working, I used to buy chocolate bars for his packed lunch, but if he found them, he would eat them in one go! I used to hide them around the house so Adam couldn't find them. But he admitted that Tio would show him where the hiding places where.

'Show me the chocolate', he'd say, and she would run off and sniff it out and show him.

She died while we were living at Model Village in Creswell, and we still miss her today.

Not long after Tio died, I saw an advert on the internet for a Jack Russell who was free to a good home from Leeds. The lady who had the dog told us she had rescued it from a neighbour who was an alcoholic and was mistreating the dog, so she was desperate to get rid of the Jack Russell before the neighbour realised.

Paul and I finished work and went all the way to Leeds to fetch the dog. The situation did seem a bit funny at the time, but I was just thinking about the poor dog. She was called Bonnie. She was really skinny, and when you stroked her, you could feel her bones. She looked awful.

We got Bonnie home late that night. She was just shaking and didn't go to sleep. We booked her to see the vet that evening and they advised us over the phone to just give her small bits of food, like chicken and fish, which we did.

In fact, she only had about one piece. The woman from Leeds told us that she had given the dog a lamb shank and sliced meat before we fetched her.

The following morning, Paul and I went to work, hoping Bonnie would be okay until I returned.

When I got home, I was getting ready to fetch Paul from work and to take the dog to the vet, but Bonnie started to wobble about and fall over. I picked her up, and she collapsed and died in my arms. I was devastated.

We still took her to the vets and explained everything to them. Bonnie was microchipped and they gave us her number to trace the original owners. And also they said that maybe the lamb shank had caused her death because, being starved, her stomach couldn't take it and caused damage to her insides.

The woman from Leeds kept texting us to ask how Bonnie was. I didn't want to upset her, as it was close to Christmas and she had kids, but she kept asking, so I told her Bonnie had died. The woman went off on one, accusing us of killing her and threatening to come to our house. Paul got in touch with the police because her threats were getting worse. They said they would send someone round to talk to her. We didn't hear anything from her again.

It turned out that the dog belonged to her boyfriend and the reason that she got so uptight was when we said the vet had the microchip number and were thinking of prosecuting the owner because of the state Bonnie was in.

The following year, we decided to have another dog. That's when we got Marley, the loopy Labrador. She's very clever but also very clumsy. She is still a puppy really, so we are hoping she calms down.

We got her from someone at Heath, near Chesterfield, who advertised her on the internet. The man's house was a bit of a mess. There was a big bird cage in the corner of the room with a parrot in it which kept squawking out. All its mess was round it on the floor. The fireplace hadn't been cleaned for months and the ash was spilling out all over the carpet. We didn't know where the carpet started and finished, it was that messy.

We were taken into the kitchen where there was a big cage with four puppies in it. The man told us that they were Red Fox Labradors. The mother of the pups was there. She looked like a golden retriever, and she was very friendly and calm.

Two of the pups were spoken for, but there was one in the litter which was a lot lighter in colour than the others – blonder.

'I'll have that one,' I said.

The man picked it up. 'Oh, I'm sorry, that one's spoken for,' he said. He knew, because it had a little patch shaved in its fur on its leg. Each pup had a different leg shaved. So he put it back in the cage and then picked another one up.

'That one's taken as well,' he said. Then he picked up the original pup that I'd chosen. 'This one's still free,' he said. I wasn't going to say anything!

When he gave us the paperwork for the dog, we worked out that he had been looking at the dogs wrong and had mixed the paperwork up too.

But it didn't matter; we took her home and called her Marley, from the film *Marley and Me*.

As you can see, the dogs are a big part of mine and Paul's lives. When I met Paul, he already had Tiger, a Staffie he got from the RSPCA.

Tiger is terrified of everything and likes to be asleep on the bed. He's just like a teenager. You shout him for his dinner, then he goes back to bed. He's ten years old now.

My Nanna always said that you could tell how a man treats a woman by how he treats a dog. Paul loves the dogs and is always having conversations with them!

Me with Simba.

Me with Scamp.

Tim the Italian Greyhound.

Max the Jack Russell, looking after Adam.

Elle and Meg.

Oscar enjoying a walk on a beach.

Oscar – a bit of a party animal!

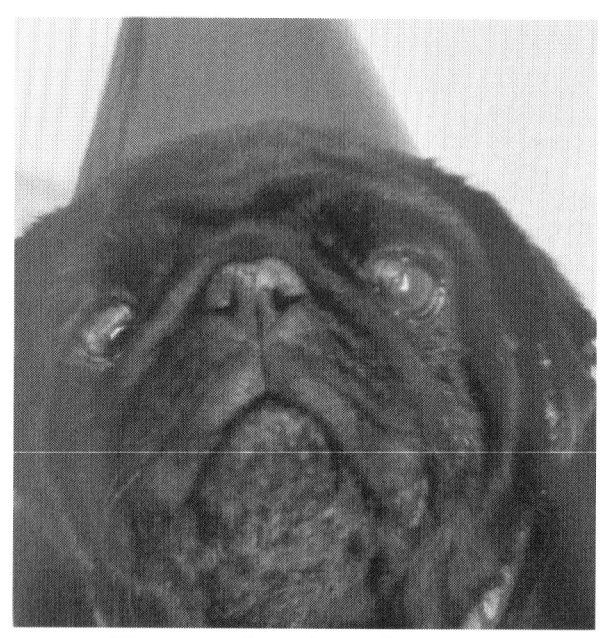

Tio – a truly unique character!

Oscar, Ellie, Tio and Tiger.

Me, Paul and Adam with Ellie, Tio and Oscar.

Tiger, the Staffie.

Poor little Bonnie.

Crazy puppy Marley.

Chapter 20: Up, Up and Away!

For my birthday this year, Paul got me a hot air balloon ride. It is something that I have always wanted to do since I was a child.

I would watch hot air balloons when I lived at Dowdeswell Street. They would land and take off from the field next to us at certain times of the year.

I always wondered what it was like to be in the basket underneath and what it you could see when you looked down.

It took us seven attempts to arrange for our flight, because the weather conditions had to be just right. But early one September morning, we were up in a hot air balloon, looking over the Derbyshire Peak District. It is a magical, wonderful landscape of quaint villages, stone houses and farms, surrounded by woodlands and a patchwork of fields. With the tops of the moors and the rugged cliffs in the distance.

We set off from Tissington village and landed in a farmer's field on the other side of Youlgrave.

It was a lovely experience and so peaceful – it's like floating on a cloud.

All your cares and worries seem to be left behind on the ground.

I would like to be friends again with some of my family. We were really close at one time. It is a shame, and I'm sorry about how things have worked out. Maybe in time, there will be a chance. I never give up hoping.

I've learnt many lessons over the years.

You should do what you have always dreamed of, whenever you have the chance to do so.

You should treat everyone with respect. Every person is different: their opinions and views, lifestyle and culture.

Never judge a book by its cover. When you meet someone, you don't know what their past or circumstances are.

Always have a smile on your face, no matter what. It brightens someone else's day and also makes others wonder what you're up to!

And my last useful lesson – get a dog, if possible! They are the most loyal and loveable friends you can have.

Everyone has a story to tell, even if it's just a chapter. I wanted to tell mine so hopefully it will help someone, even if it's just one person, to know that whatever happens, you can survive. Never give up hope.

It will make you a stronger, wiser and that bit more of a special person.

I don't know what life will throw at me in the coming days, months or years, but as I look across at Paul, I know for sure that he will be there to support me, and I know that we can overcome anything together.

I am lucky after all.

Up, up and away!

The End

Or is it?!?

Help and Advice

SAMARITANS

www.samaritans.org
Call: 116 123
Email: jo@samaritans.org
Write: Chris
 Freepost RSRB- KKBY- CYJK
 PO Box 9090
 Stirling
 FK8 2SA

Samaritans is a unique charity dedicated to reducing feelings of isolation and disconnection which can lead to suicide. They respond to a call for help every six seconds. They are there 24/7.

WOMEN'S AID

https://www.womensaid.org.uk
Live chat: https://chat.womensaid.org.uk/
Email: helpline@womensaid.org.uk

National Domestic Violence Helpline (24-hours)
Call: 0808 2000 247. Runs in partnership with Refuge. If you think you might be in danger, call the police immediately on 999.

Women's Aid provides life-saving services and builds a future where domestic violence is not tolerated.

Everything is strictly confidential and the person's safety is their priority.

MIND

www.mind.org.uk

MIND provides advice and support to anyone experiencing a mental health problem. They campaign to improve services, raise awareness and promote understanding.

CRUSE BEREAVEMENT CARE

https://www.cruse.org.uk

Call: 0808 808 1677 (Mon-Fri 9am-5pm).

This charity provides support for people after the death of someone close to them.

VICTIM SUPPORT

https://www.victimsupport.org.uk

Call: 0808 168 9111 (24 hour helpline).

Victim Support offers help to people affected by crime or traumatic events. It aims to make them feel safer and find the strength to move on.

LIFESIGNS

www.lifesigns.org.uk

Self-harm guidance and support. Lifesigns is a small user-led charity, creating understanding about self-injury. It is their mission to guide people who hurt themselves towards new ways of coping, when they are ready for the journey.

BUTTERFLY PROJECT

Email: butterflyproject.contact@gmail.com

The Butterfly Project runs self-harm support groups for 13-17s and over 18's. The Butterfly Project aims to provide members with a tool box of positive coping strategies, in a non-judgemental and friendly environment.

They also be found on social media, at

Facebook:
https://www.facebook.com/Thebtrflyproject/

Twitter: https://twitter.com/btrflyproject

BULLYING UK

www.bullying.co.uk

Call: 0808 800 2222

Bullying UK provides help and support for a wide range of bullying issues. From bullying in school or the work place, to cyber bullying.

More Help

To find other charities and organisations for help go to:
https://helplines.org/helplines/

Other Useful Information

"Ask for Angela". This is a safety campaign now running in most parts of the UK. If you are out on a

date and feel uncomfortable or threatened, you can go to the bar and "ask for Angela". Then staff will then phone for a taxi or help you leave discreetly.
There's more information on the National Pubwatch website:
https://www.nationalpubwatch.org.uk/news/national-pubwatch-supports-ask-angela-campaign/

Hollie Guard App: This is a smartphone app, designed to help you to stay safe.
A simple shake or tap activates Hollie Guard, automatically sending your location and audio/video evidence to your designated contacts. For more information and to download the app, go to www.hollieguard.com

What3Words App: This is a geocode system you can download onto smartphones. If you are lost, the app will pinpoint exactly where you are and it makes it easy for you to be found by your friends, family and the emergency services. Download the app and find more information at: www.what3words.com

There are other apps available with similar ideas to keep you safe. It is a good idea for everyone to have some kind of personal safety app on their phone.
　　Even if you don't think that you will need it, it's there for you and your loved ones' peace of mind, knowing you have some sort of safety net if something does happen.

I can't tell you when,
But I can promise you,
It will get better,
It will get easier
And it will all be worthwhile
Just promise me
You will never give up.

Email: lisabroughauthor@gmail.com

Printed in Poland
by Amazon Fulfillment
Poland Sp. z o.o., Wrocław